AN EXHIBITION IN CELEBRATION OF THE 250TH ANNIVERSARY OF HIS BIRTH

PUBLICATION MADE POSSIBLE BY A GRANT FROM UNITED TECHNOLOGIES CORPORATION

G. Washington

A FIGURE UPON THE STAGE

BY MARGARET BROWN KLAPTHOR &
HOWARD ALEXANDER MORRISON

DIVISION OF POLITICAL HISTORY

NATIONAL MUSEUM OF AMERICAN HISTORY,
SMITHSONIAN INSTITUTION,
WASHINGTON, D. C. 1982

THE SMITHSONIAN INSTITUTION PRESS

Library of Congress Cataloging in Publication Data

Klapthor, Margaret Brown.
 G. Washington, a figure upon the stage.

 Supt. of Docs. no.: SI 1.2:W27
 1. Washington, George, 1732-1799 — Museums, relics, etc. —
 Exhibitions.
 I. Morrison, Howard Alexander.
 II. National Museum of American History (U.S.)
 III. Smithsonian Institution.
 IV. Title.
E312.5.K56   973.4'1'0924   [B] 81-607124   AACR2
ISBN O-87474-592-6
ISBN O-87474-593-4 (pbk.)

Catalog edited by Carole J. Jacobs
Designed by Derek Birdsall

This book was produced by the Smithsonian Institution Press,
Washington, D.C., and printed by Garamond Pridemark Press,
Baltimore, Maryland.

Exhibit at the National Museum of American History,
February 22, 1982 — January 7, 1983

Exhibition by: Margaret B. Klapthor, Curator
Howard A. Morrison, Museum Technician

Research and technical assistance:
Carolyn P. Davies
Herbert R. Collins
Barbara J. Coffee
William L. Bird Jr.
Donald E. Kloster
Anne W. Murray
George T. Sharrer
William S. Pretzer
& the George Washington Task Force

Exhibit designer: Nadya A. Makovenyi

Project Manager: Douglas E. Evelyn

TABLE OF CONTENTS

PREFACE

FOREWORD

LENDERS TO THE EXHIBITION

PART I:
"TO SIT LIKE PATIENCE ON A MONUMENT"

PART II:
"TAKING CARE TO PERFORM THE PARTS ASSIGNED"

The photographs in this catalog were provided by the following persons and institutions:

The Adirondack Museum, **figure 8;** *the Boston Athenaeum,* **figure 102;** *Thomas C. Bradshaw,* **figures 85, 87;** *Buffalo and Erie County Historical Society,* **figure 137;** *Clements Library,* **figure 151;** *James R. Dunlop, Inc.,* **figure 143;** *Edison Institute,* **figure 39;** *Embassy of Venezuela,* **figure 159;** *Fasch Studios,* **figure 158;** *George Fistrovich,* **figure 3;** *Fred Fried,* **figure 27;** *Helga Photo,* **figure 76;** *Henry Francis du Pont Winterthur Museum,* **figure 131;** *Edgar Hinchcliffe,* **figure 72;** *The Historical Society of Pennsylvania,* **figure 123;** *Huntington Galleries,* **figure 26;** *Huntington Library,* **figure 101;** *John Carter Brown Library,* **figure 79;** *Stephen Kovacik,* **figure 80;** *The Library Company of Philadelphia,* **figure 153;** *Maryland Historical Society,* **figure 122;** *Richard Merrill,* **figure 46;** *Mount Vernon Ladies' Association of the Union,* **figures 86, 88;** *National Archives and Records Service,* **figure 128;** *National Gallery (London),* **figure 82;** *National Gallery of Art,* **figures 4, 145;** *National Portrait Gallery,* **figure 144;** *The New-York Historical Society,* **figures 108, 139;** *New York Public Library,* **figure 141;** *Charles Phillips,* **figures 6, 9, 11, 12, 14, 16, 17, 22, 33, 34, 35, 40, 41, 42, 43, 44, 62, 65, 67, 68, 69, 70, 73, 74, 77, 78, 84, 89, 90, 91, 96, 98, 99, 106, 107, 110, 112, 113, 116, 117, 118, 120, 121, 125, 135, 138, 140, 142, 148, 154, 156, 157;** *Photoworld,* **figure 54;** *The Pierpont Morgan Library,* **figure 114;** *Smithsonian Institution Photographic Services Division,* **figures 1, 2, 5, 7, 10, 13, 15, 18, 19, 20, 21, 24, 28, 29, 30, 31, 32, 36, 37, 38, 45, 47, 48, 49, 50, 51, 52, 53, 55, 56, 57, 58, 59, 60, 61, 63, 64, 66, 71, 75, 83, 92, 93, 94, 95, 97, 100, 103, 104, 105, 109, 111, 115, 124, 127, 129, 130, 132, 133, 134, 136, 146, 149, 150, 152, 155;** *The Society of the Cincinnati,* **figure 106;** *John Tennant,* **figure 25;** *U. S. Naval Academy Museum,* **figure 23;** *Washington and Lee University,* **figure 81;** *West Point Museum,* **figure 119.**

We are proud to join in partnership with the National Museum of American History to produce this handsome volume as a memorial to one of our nation's towering heroes. We hope the book gives much pleasure to the American public.

Harry J. Gray
Chairman and Chief Executive Officer
United Technologies Corporation

PREFACE

The Smithsonian Institution is custodian of two important collections of Washington memorabilia. One came from the Lewis family in direct descent from Eleanor Parke Custis Lewis, granddaughter of Martha Washington and adopted child of Mount Vernon, and the other from the Peter family in direct descent from Martha Parke Custis Peter, also a granddaughter of Martha Washington.

Important pieces had been added from other private collectors to these rich holdings through the years. As there had been no major George Washington exhibition in many years, and never one by the Smithsonian Institution, it seemed appropriate to suggest that we present an exhibition which would assess George Washington—both the myth and the man —in terms of modern historiography.

The idea for such an exhibition germinated many years ago in the mind of this curator. After discussing the concept with colleagues in the ensuing years and suggesting such an exhibition informally, I prepared a formal exhibit proposal which outlined a presentation of George Washington as a man who definitively reflected the values and customs of his century, social class, community, and family through objects, documents, and contemporary pictorial material intimately associated with him. The proposal was submitted for the Department of National History by Dr. Vladimir Clain-Stefanelli, Chairman, in 1978.

As we studied the man, my colleagues and I—especially Howard Morrison who joined me in 1980—came to understand Washington's own appreciation of the importance of style in creating a public image. Much of his success can be traced to his cultivation of style and his skill in adopting the style proper to a particular occasion. Washington shared Shakespeare's perception that "all the world's a stage and all the men and women in it players," as is documented in his own words. Like many of his contemporaries, he saw the great events taking place in the New World as "theater." Hence, the title of the exhibit.

Washington was so successful at playing his role that the man became a monument in his own time. Succeeding generations ascribed to this monument qualities which fulfilled their own needs, so that the image of Washington reflects a microcosm of nineteenth and twentieth century American society. The collections of this Museum are rich in objects which illuminate the changing constituent attitudes of ongoing public adulation of George Washington.

Since the proposal for this exhibit was formally submitted,

it has survived changing Directors and administrative structure within the Museum. The support of Dr. Otto Mayr during his year as Acting Director of the National Museum of History and Technology, now the National Museum of American History, was critical to the survival of the proposal. We are especially grateful to Mr. Roger G. Kennedy, Director since 1979, whose personal enthusiasm eventually made the proposal a reality. Those of us who worked on the exhibit are indebted to him for sharing with us his knowledge and experience at a formative stage and for his contribution to and support of the final organizational script of the exhibit. The members of the George Washington Task Force, formed by Mr. Kennedy, also deserve recognition for contributions at a formative stage.

Outside the Museum, the cooperation of the Mount Vernon Ladies' Association of the Union was crucial to the success of our show. Special recognition is due to the staff at Mount Vernon, especially John Castellani, Director; Christine Meadows, Curator; Ellen MacAllister, Librarian; and John Rhodehamel, Archivist.

As the exhibition developed, advice and counsel were provided by Dr. Marcus Cunliffe, The George Washington University, Washington, D.C.; Dr. Merrill Peterson, National Humanities Center, Research Triangle Park, North Carolina; Dr. Thaddeus W. Tate Jr., Institute of Early American Culture, Williamsburg, Virginia; and the editorial staff of The Papers of George Washington, Charlottesville, Virginia. Miss Dorothy Twohig, Associate Editor of The Papers, was especially helpful at every stage of the preparation of the script. Thanks are extended not only for ourselves, but for all the millions who will see and learn from this exhibit.

The support of the Library of Congress was also essential, and we would like to especially thank Dr. Paul Sifton and Mr. C.F.W. Coker of the Division of Manuscripts for their interest and cooperation. The work of Jon D. Freshour, Registrar of the Exhibits Office of the Library, has also been helpful to the final production.

The assistance and enthusiasm of Mr. Clement Conger, Curator of The White House, and of the Registrar, Miss Betty Monkman, resulted in the inclusion of outstanding objects from The White House to the exhibition.

Other people who helped us secure the objects we needed to round out the exhibition and who deserve our thanks are the Honorable Thomas P. (Tip) O'Neill Jr., Speaker of the House of Representatives, and Mr. Gary G. Hymel, then-Administrative Assistant to the Speaker; Mr. George White, Architect of the Capitol; Mr. John Kilbourne, Director of the Museum of the

Society of the Cincinnati; Mrs. Jean Frederico, Director of the Museum of the National Society of the Daughters of the American Revolution; Mr. Edgar Hinchcliffe, Historian of Appleby School, Cumbria, England; Mr. James Hoofnagle, Clerk of the Court of Fairfax County; Mr. Marvin Fowler, Curator of the George Washington National Masonic Memorial, Alexandria, Virginia; Sir Michael Levey, Director, National Gallery, London, England; and Mr. Richard Kuehne, Curator, the West Point Museum.

This exhibit would not have been possible without the help of every curatorial and service department in the National Museum of American History. Acknowledgment is made to the consistently fine service of the Registrar's Office, the Objects Processing Facility, the Conservation Division, and the Building Manager and his staff.

The design of the exhibit was done by Nadya Makovenyi, who shared with us the responsibility of turning concept into reality. Credit for production goes to the Exhibits Production staff, National Museum of American History; for editing the script to Michael P. Fruitman, Office of Exhibits Central; and for the excellent photography to the Office of Printing and Photographic Services under its director, James H. Wallace. This catalog has been patiently shepherded to completion by Josiah Hatch and his staff.

Coordinating the project was the responsibility of Douglas E. Evelyn, Deputy Director of the National Museum of American History. Mr. Evelyn's enthusiasm and assistance have been a major factor in meeting and solving the problems which are always part of any major museum exhibition.

Within the Museum a special acknowledgment is due to Craddock Goins, Curator, and Donald Kloster, Associate Curator, of the Division of Military History for their work on the section of the exhibition relating to George Washington as the Virginia Colonel and the Commander in Chief of the Continental Army. Terry Sharrer, Associate Curator of Extractive Industries, provided script and located objects for the sections of the exhibition which pertain to agriculture in Virginia during the eras of Augustine Washington and of George Washington.

The staff of the Division of Political History deserves special acknowledgment for support and contributions to all phases of this undertaking. Herbert R. Collins and Edith P. Mayo, my fellow curators, have been generous with their knowledge and have made significant suggestions in every area of the exhibition. Mr. Collins' knowledge of Virginia history and Presidential history has been especially helpful, and Ms. Mayo's assistance with the area devoted to the monumentalization of

George Washington was instrumental to the structure of this section. Barbara J. Coffee, acting as coordinator of all activities relating to the objects selected for the exhibition, was a vital member of the team which worked on this exhibition. Marilyn V. Higgins' knowledge of forms and procedures for loans from other museums eased this important detail. William L. Bird Jr. provided thoughtful and competent assistance with the area devoted to the Presidency and located significant objects to illustrate the themes he had identified. Carolyn P. Davies, who first came to us as an intern to work on the exhibition, produced research papers on many areas of the Washington story. Hours of leg-work spent in transporting objects to the staging area, to photography, conservation and production, and more hours spent in filling out forms for exhibition and catalog notebooks have made her a valuable member of the team who produced this exhibition and catalog.

To Eleanor L. Boyne, secretary of the Division, goes my heartfelt thanks for her devotion to every detail of the project. Her skill as a typist has contributed to every phase of the production of the exhibition and the catalog. Her personal interest and knowledge prompted her to make many arrangements that relieved the rest of the staff of hours of work. She was quick to spot embarrassing discrepancies in the text as she typed script and catalog.

The National Museum of American History and all who read and enjoy this catalog owe United Technologies Corporation a tribute of thanks for its assistance, which permitted us to publish it in a style worthy of George Washington. Derek Birdsall's insightful reading of the manuscript produced a catalog design which is as responsive to the nature of the exhibit as it is visually splendid.

I leave my colleague, Howard A. Morrison, to the last because it is hard to find words to say thank you to one who has worked side by side with me for the past two years, sharing every burden and frustration as well as every joy of producing a major exhibition. His scholarly input into the final product, its theme, its organization, and the words in which our ideas are expressed deserves recognition not only from me, but from this Museum and from the many people who will see the exhibit and read the catalog. To Howard I say, in the words of George Washington, "I [have] felt all that love, respect and attachment for you, with which length of years, close connexion and your merits have inspired me."

Margaret Brown Klapthor
Curator
Division of Political History

George Washington's life filled the middle and final thirds of the eighteenth century, and closed with the century in December 1799. He had been notable in his own Virginia since the mid-1750s, and throughout America after he took command of the colonies' armed forces in June 1775. From then on, indeed, Washington was famous around the world. Americans might disagree with one another about many things, and disagree even more with foreigners. Belief in the greatness of General (or President) Washington was, however, one theme they could nearly always unite upon.

Tributes therefore began to pour in upon him long before his death. His birthday (February 22 or, according to the old unreformed calendar, February 11) was already assuming the status of a national holiday. In the nineteenth century, anniversaries of his birth, or of his inauguration as president (April 1789) were increasingly prominent public rituals. Thus, at the semi-centennial of his presidential inauguration, in 1839, the tributes included a two-hour speech from ex-President John Quincy Adams and a special ode composed by the well-known poet William Cullen Bryant. At the 1889 centennial gala in New York City, President Benjamin Harrison actually stood in for Washington; Harrison restaged the taking of the oath of office before a jostling crowd of a million in the streets near Broadway and Wall, where the original ceremony had taken place in the presence of a mere few thousand people. The 1932 bicentennial of Washington's birth, masterminded by the tireless Congressman Sol Bloom, was a patriotic extravaganza that ran on for months. One of Bloom's schemes was to supply every classroom in the land with a reproduction of Gilbert Stuart's "Athenaeum" portrait of Washington. Another bold promotional event of the bicentennial involved the flamboyant aviator Jimmy Doolittle. Between dawn and dark on July 25, 1932, Doolittle flew 2600 miles, covering every part of the United States where George Washington had set foot. Miss Anne Madison Washington, a middle-aged great-great-great grandniece of the General, sportingly accompanied Doolittle and declared she had enjoyed every minute of what was for her a maiden flight. Doolittle also carried a cargo of mailbags, dropping them off at various points to dramatize the possibilities of airmail delivery.

Hero-worship was an obvious feature of these bygone occasions. Their odes and orations presented George Washington as a person of well-nigh perfect virtue and attainment. Ralph Waldo Emerson, who acquired a copy of the Stuart portrait in 1849, said: "The head of Washington hangs in my dining-room ... and I cannot keep my eyes off it. It has a certain Appalachian strength, as if it were truly the first-fruits of America and expressed the Country. The heavy, leaden eyes turn on you, as the eyes of an ox in a pasture. And the mouth has gravity and depth of quiet, as if this MAN had absorbed all the serenity of America, and left none for his rickety, hysterical countrymen." A few years later, in conversation with the sculptor Hiram Powers, the novelist Nathaniel Hawthorne discussed the problem of depicting George Washington three-dimensionally. Another sculptor, Horatio Greenough, had been ridiculed for his giant figure of Washington seated in a toga in the guise of Zeus. Powers like Greenough appreciated the "ideality" that could be evoked by means of unclad classical forms. But Hawthorne, displaying the ordinary layman's taste of his day, thought Powers crazy even to contemplate a nude version of the "Pater Patriae." "Did anybody ever see Washington naked! It is inconceivable. He had no nakedness, but I imagine, was born with his clothes on and his hair powdered, and made a stately bow on his first appearance in the world." Hawthorne's image reminds us of the elegant little child-adult in Grant Wood's delightful version of young George and the cherry tree, as envisaged by Parson Weems. Their Washington was not only never nude, but somehow never a boy either.

Hawthorne and Powers did agree, though, in attributing to their hero the kind of awesome personality Emerson had sensed from staring at the Stuart portrait. The sculptor, who at the time was executing portrait busts at his studio in Florence, Italy, remarked that all European royalty "have a certain look that distinguishes them from other people, and is seen in individuals of no lower rank." Powers added that Washington was the only American to possess this look. The idea interested Hawthorne. Such people, he mused, "put themselves under glass, as it were, . . . so that . . . they keep themselves within a sort of Sanctity, and repel you by an invisible barrier. Even if they invite you, with a show of warmth and hospitality, you cannot get through. I, too, recognize this look in the portraits of Washington; in him, a mild, benevolent coldness and apartness," indicating a "formality which seems to have been deeper in him than in any other mortal, and which built up an actual fortification between himself and human sympathy." Hawthorne wished that "for once, Washington could come out of his envelopment, and show us what his real dimensions were."

Emerson, Hawthorne, Powers: each in one way or another spoke for the creative imagination. None had ever met or seen George Washington. Each chose to interpret the General so as to uphold some theory of human behavior. It does not follow that their collective notion of Washington told the whole truth, or revealed much more than a mid-nineteenth century conception of the nation's patriot leader. Hawthorne's final comment

in fact suggests he felt there was, behind the fortification, a "real" Washington whose temperament might be as surprising as that of some complex character in a Hawthorne story.

Certainly the biographers of the twentieth century have been at pains to explore what may lie behind the exterior of the hero-giant and the myths that have accrued about him. Thus, Douglas Southall Freeman's multi-volume study was able to show that Washington the young Virginian was restless, ambitious, anxious to please, and sometimes hard or aggressive in his dealings. Another scholar, Bernhard Knollenberg, argued quite persuasively that at least in the early stages of the War of Independence, Washington made errors of generalship; and that while he profited from them, he was also inclined to shift the blame onto others, as well as to regard criticism as a personal slur. During the anxious period that culminated in the so-called Conway "Cabal," or plot to undermine their leader, we may wonder with Knollenberg why Congress or some of the other generals should not have fastened responsibility on Washington. He was commander in chief. If he could claim credit for success, should he not be at least potentially blameable for lack of success?

Again, Washington used to be lavishly praised for his refusal to accept any financial return for his services, other than reimbursement for specified expenses. The humorist Marvin Kitman has in recent years correctly stated that General Washington did as a result receive more money from Congress than if he had, like every other Continental officer, merely been given a fixed salary. Exercising the humorist's right to exaggerate, Mr. Kitman goes further, maintaining that Washington should be seen as Founding Father of the great American sport of expense account padding. What Kitman is not able to demonstrate is that Washington's claims were fraudulent or greedy, or that fair-minded contemporaries believed they were. In comparison with the heads of state of his own era, or the commanders and chief executives of ours, Washington was recompensed on a most frugal scale.

Still, sober academics have in effect agreed with Kitman, in drawing attention to the amount of hostile comment directed at President Washington, especially during his second administration. Most of this came from journalists in the Jeffersonian Republican camp. Most of their allegations—including the charge that he was overspending his salary allowance, and drawing upon it in advance of authorization—may be discounted as partisan spleen. On the other hand, current historical interpretation does tend to emphasize that Washington was himself finally a partisan, on the Federalist side of the fierce controversies of the 1790s. His lofty impartiality begins to look somewhat different in this light. The newest major biographer, James T. Flexner, clearly acknowledges the greatness of the man, yet stops short of fulsome tribute. For example, he touches on a subject that would have been taboo in the drawing-rooms of Hawthorne's day: the failure of Washington to sire children by Martha Custis. Martha had borne offspring before being widowed in a previous marriage. She was therefore fertile: was the General? Flexner revives an old supposition, not found in genteel biographies, that Washington might have been rendered sterile by an attack of some youthful illness such as mumps.

Flexner is fairly explicit on other physical aspects, including Washington's poor teeth (only one of which remained to him by 1789, when he became president), and his perhaps poorer dentures. These clumsy discolored fitments, improvised out of hippopotamus ivory and metal, almost seem enough in themselves to account for the stories of George Washington's lack of sparkle at dinner parties. He must have endured years of embarrassing discomfort with them.

Flexner also dwells on Washington's decline in vitality during the 1790s, with the implication that the president felt increasingly old and weary, and more inclined to fuss over inessentials. The argument is not that Washington had become senile: he was spared the sad fate that overtook his one-time rival, the British King George III, who in old age went blind and lost his memory. Nevertheless, we are given glimpses of a fatigued and harassed statesman, glad to escape the burdens of office and convinced that, since the Washingtons were not a long-lived family, he would not survive many more years.

Such interpretations of George Washington are without animosity. They display none of the malice apparent in "debunking" biographies of the 1920's by W.E. Woodward and Rupert Hughes. What the newer analyses do strive for is a more realistic view of Washington in his own time and place. The cruder sort of heroic biography tended to place him so prominently in the foreground that everything else in his era was dwarfed and out of focus.

The National Museum of American History's 1982 exhibit "G. Washington: A Figure Upon the Stage" offers an important corrective to such bygone distortion. Here are assembled a large number of artifacts acquired and used by Washington — probably a larger quantity than has ever before been brought together. They are related to their owner's actual circumstances as surveyor, farmer, huntsman, soldier, burgess, magistrate, vestryman, freemason. In other words, we are reminded that despite his dignified reserve, George Washington was a man of his day, an eighteenth-century Virginian. He was a social being,

with a wide range of activities and obligations. He would not have been as effective a leader had he not been so thoroughly attuned to the life and thought of the American colonies. His contemporaries recognized him as an authority because he palpably knew what he was talking about. To people in Virginia he was among other things an enterprising experimenter with crops and fertilizers, a speculator in land, a businessman prompt to discharge his debts and expecting others to do the same, a keen judge of horseflesh, a mule-breeder, a member of committees, an attender of dances and theatrical performances, a conscientious subscriber to worthy causes.

This emphasis is healthy. To portray Washington, or any American hero, as a superman is to misrepresent the attitudes of a nation which, from the outset, expressed a determination not to be ruled or reigned over by remote, superior beings, but instead to be governed for strictly limited periods of time by elected citizens, whose authority was thus brief and probationary.

Moreover, the emphasis helps to rescue Washington from another fate: the tendency, apparent for instance in Major Doolittle's spectacular flight, to exploit Washington's exploits. This exploitation has many aspects. Some of them have a long history. For example, the Federalists created political clubs which they disguised as patriotic groups under the name of Washington Benevolent Societies. They hoped to gain votes for themselves and cast doubt upon the Americanism of their political rivals, the Jeffersonian Republicans. A generation later, the new temperance movement called itself "Washingtonian" in a bid for nationwide support. The American or Know-Nothing party of the 1850s adapted a supposed Revolutionary War order of Washington's ("Put none but Americans on guard tonight") to lend respectability to their nativist campaigns against the foreign-born. Sometimes the linkage was harmless, as in the attempt of various religious denominations to prove that George Washington admired or had even joined their faith. Sometimes it was justified, as with the pride shown by Masons in Washington's affiliation: he was in truth a member of their order. And sometimes the exploitation has been unashamedly commercial, as in the annual consumers' rite of Washington's Birthday sales.

Yet no matter how hard we try, it may prove impossible to separate the "real" Washington from the legends that have grown up around him. Mason Locke Weems produced anecdotes about young George, especially the story of the hatchet and the cherry tree, that are usually regarded as absurd inventions, perhaps best treated with the indulgent humor implicit in the painting by Grant Wood. But was Weems such a liar? It is worth remembering that he was an Episcopal parson; that while he was never "Rector of Mount Vernon" (a title he was fond of announcing), he did know Washington, and even once stayed overnight at Mount Vernon; and that his biography was published only a few years after Washington's death. Moreover, despite Grant Wood's charming portrayal, Weems did not mean to suggest that Washington emerged from the cradle an instant, priggish grown-up. On the contrary: Weems' aim was to present a credible person—someone who had been a normal, high-spirited child, capable of mischief, guided along the right paths by his father and other firm if genial mentors. Weems was reacting against the big "official" biography written by Chief Justice John Marshall. Marshall, a fellow-Virginian, was much closer to George Washington than Weems had ever been. But Weems complained with some truth that Marshall's book was deadly dull because it lacked the homely, personal touch. Thomas Jefferson disliked Marshall's biography for different motives. Jefferson's complaint was that Marshall, in equating Washington with everything statemanlike and honorable, in effect condemned as unpatriotic anyone who ventured to question Washington administration policies.

Where in this is the "real" man? We have seen that Emerson, Hawthorne, and Hiram Powers held decided opinions on how the character of Washington ought to be interpreted. They had more or less opted for the notion of Washington as an eighteenth-century Virginia gentleman. Yet neither they nor their contemporaries were absolutely sure this was an appropriate model for a bustling democratic nation. In commentary like theirs, odd hesitancies are apparent. Thus, as some nineteenth-century Northerners worried, Washington had been a Southern aristocrat, a large slaveholder, and connected through Martha Washington and the Custis family to Robert E. Lee, the leader of the Confederate "rebels." "Shall we," asked the New England abolitionist-clergyman Theodore Parker, "build him a great monument, founding it in a slave pen?" True, Washington's will stipulated that his slaves should be freed. But did this make him democratic, on the level of an Abraham Lincoln?

Praise of Washington seems perfunctory and minimal in such assessments as this, drawn from "Important Events of the Century" (a compilation produced for the 1876 centennial): "His inherited wealth was great, and the antiquity of his family gave him high social rank. On his Potomac farms he had hundreds of slaves, and at his Mount Vernon home he was like the prince of a wide domain, free from dependence or restraint. He was fond of equipage and the appurtenances of high life. . . . This generous style of living, added perhaps to his native reserve, exposed him to the charge of aristocratic feeling. . . . His manner was formal and dignified. He was more solid than brilliant, and had more judgment than genius. He had great dread of public life, cared little for books, and had no library." Inaccurate, slapdash journalese, of course, not typical of the mass of testimony on Washington. But there are similar indications that Americans were either no longer awed by Washington, or not entirely at ease in saluting him. The writer William Dean Howells, describing the 1876 Philadelphia centennial exposition for the "Atlantic Monthly," commended the display of Washington clothes and "other personal relics, like his camp-bed, his table furniture, his sword, his pistols, and so forth . . . ." But then Howells playfully rebukes the organizers for "the language of the placard on the clothes of the Father of his Country," which "now reads 'Coat, Vest, and Pants of George Washington,' whereas it is his honored waistcoat which is meant, and his buckskin breeches. . . ." If this detail reached Howell's friend Mark Twain, we can be fairly sure Twain would have relished the man-to-man monosyllables of the Centennial label. And behind such healthy irreverence, perhaps, lies the old idea—voiced during Washington's lifetime—that the Father of his Country did after all display judgment rather than genius, and was not the most sparkling of companions at dinner.

So did his countrymen truly know how to treat Washington? His home was in sad decay on the eve of the Civil War, and only rescued by valiant private efforts, especially those of the Mount Vernon Ladies' Association. Work on his monument ceased during the 1850s, when it was a stump less than a third of its projected height. Construction was not resumed until considerably after the Civil War, and the Monument was not completed until 1885.

On the other hand we must reckon with the recurrent anniversary ceremonials, the whole vast volume of adulatory recognition. The point is that, during Washington's lifetime and ever since, Americans have sought a middle way between proper regard and highfalutin gush. They rightly feel he was exceptional. They rightly hesitate to turn him into a demigod—demigods not being allowed for in the Constitution. They alternate accordingly, as with each of Washington's presidential successors, between near-adoration and near-contempt. At this distance from his era, the problem is interesting rather than perplexing. He has been absorbed and diffused into his nation. This makes him unique: no other president, no other American, had undergone so prodigious a metamorphosis. George Washington is also, however, a man of the eighteenth century; and, thanks to the skill of archivists and curators, a significant part of that era can be reconstituted for us. Here are the man and the monument, mingled yet distinguishable.

LENDERS TO THE EXHIBITION

The Adirondack Museum, Blue Mountain Lake, New York
Alexandria-Washington Lodge No. 22, A.F. & A.M., Alexandria, Virginia
American Antiquarian Society, Worcester, Massachusetts
Babcock Galleries, New York, New York
William L. Bird Jr., Washington, D.C.
Board of Regents, Gunston Hall, Lorton, Virginia
Eleanor L. Boyne, Springfield, Virginia
Boy Scouts of America, Dallas, Texas
Buffalo and Erie County Historical Society, Buffalo, New York
Clements Library, University of Michigan, Ann Arbor, Michigan
Herbert R. Collins, Arlington, Virginia
Colonial Williamsburg, Williamsburg, Virginia
Daughters of the American Revolution Museum, Washington, D.C.
Carolyn P. Davies, Arlington, Virginia
Edison Institute, Henry Ford Museum & Greenfield Village, Dearborn, Michigan
E. J. Kupjack Associates, Inc., Park Ridge, Illinois
Fairfax County Clerk of the Court, Fairfax, Virginia
John F. Fleming, New York, New York
The General Washington Inn, Fredericksburg, Virginia
George Washington Birthplace National Monument, Wakefield, Virginia
George Washington Memorial Parkway, U.S. National Park Service, McLean, Virginia
George Washington National Masonic Memorial, Alexandria, Virginia
The George Washington University Permanent Collection, The Dimock Gallery, Washington, D.C.
The Grammar School, Appleby, Cumbria, England
Henry Francis du Pont Winterthur Museum, Winterthur, Delaware
The Historical Society of Delaware, Wilmington, Delaware
The Historical Society of Pennsylvania, Philadelphia, Pennsylvania
Stephen William Cooper Holbrook, Arlington, Virginia
Huntington Galleries, Huntington, West Virginia
The John Carter Brown Library, Brown University, Providence, Rhode Island
The Kenmore Association, Fredericksburg, Virginia
The Library Company of Philadelphia, Philadelphia, Pennsylvania
The Library of the Boston Athenaeum, Boston, Massachusetts
Library of Congress, Washington, D.C.
Maryland Historical Society, Baltimore, Maryland
Mary Washington House, Fredericksburg, Virginia
Massachusetts Historical Society, Boston, Massachusetts
Howard A. Morrison, Washington, D.C.
Morristown National Historical Park, Morristown, New Jersey

Mount Vernon Ladies' Association of the Union, Mount Vernon, Virginia

Museo Bolivariano, Caracas, Venezuela, through the courtesy of the Embassy of Venezuela, Washington, D.C.

Museum of the American China Trade, Milton, Massachusetts

Museum of the City of New York, New York, New York

National Agricultural Library, Beltsville, Maryland

National Archives and Records Service, Washington, D.C.

National Gallery, London, England

National Gallery of Art, Washington, D.C.

National Museum of American Art, Smithsonian Institution, Washington, D.C.

National Portrait Gallery, Smithsonian Institution, Washington, D.C.

National Society of the Colonial Dames of America, Washington, D.C.

The New-York Historical Society, New York, New York

New York Public Library, New York, New York

Jack D. Parker, Sepulveda, California

Perelman Antique Toy Museum, Philadelphia, Pennsylvania

The Pierpont Morgan Library, New York, New York

Pohick Episcopal Church, Lorton, Virginia

Rhode Island Department of Economic Development, Providence, Rhode Island

Sears, Roebuck and Co., Chicago, Illinois

Shenandoah Valley National Bank, Winchester, Virginia

The Society of the Cincinnati, Washington, D.C.

Mrs. Russell R. Taylor, Greensboro, Alabama

Phillip H. Tuseth, Bay, Arkansas

United States Capitol, Washington, D.C.

University of Pennsylvania, Philadelphia, Pennsylvania

U.S. Naval Academy Museum, Annapolis, Maryland

Virginia Society, Daughters of the American Revolution, Richmond, Virginia

Virginia State Library, Richmond, Virginia

Washington and Lee University, Lexington, Virginia

Washington Bank, Washington, D.C.

Washington New Town Development Corporation, Washington, England

Wayside Inn Since 1797, Middletown, Virginia

West Point Museum Collections, U.S. Military Academy, West Point, New York

The White House, Washington, D.C.

Woodlawn Plantation, National Trust for Historic Preservation, Mount Vernon, Virginia

SOME RELEVANT BOOKS

The six volumes of Douglas Southall Freeman's *George Washington* (New York, 1948-54), covering the period to 1793, were joined by a seventh, *George Washington: First in Peace* (1957), finished after Freeman's death by his associates John A. Carroll and Mary W. Ashworth. James T. Flexner's *George Washington* (4 vols., Boston, 1965-72) is available in an abridged edition as *The Indispensable Man* (1974). Rupert Hughes' old, incomplete three-volume study appeared in 1926-30; William E. Woodward's debunking *George Washington, The Image and the Man*, came out in 1926. Marvin Kitman's book is entitled *George Washington's Expense Account* (New York, 1970). For sharp comment on military affairs, see Bernhard Knollenberg, *Washington and the Revolution: A Reappraisal* (New York, 1941). Marcus Cunliffe, *George Washington: Man and Monument* (Boston, 1958), is available in a revised paperback edition (New York, 1982).

Studies of Washington in myth and symbol include Dixon Wecter, *The Hero in America* (New York, 1941); Daniel J. Boorstin, *The Americans: The National Experience* (New York, 1965); Laurence J. Friedman, *Inventors of the Promised Land* (New York, 1975); and Michael Kammen, *A Season of Youth: The American Revolution and the Historical Imagination* (New York, 1978). See also Marcus Cunliffe, ed., Mason Locke Weems' *Life of Washington* (Cambridge, Mass., 1962), and his introduction to a new reprint of John Marshall's *Washington* (New York, 1981).

Marcus Cunliffe

A NOTE ON THE TEXT

Quoted phrases within object descriptions appear in italic type. All quoted passages are faithful to the originals, including non-standard or archaic spelling and punctuation.

PART I

G. Washington

"TO SIT LIKE PATIENCE ON A MONUMENT"

"TO SIT LIKE PATIENCE ON A MONUMENT"

In 1776 an angry mob tore down the statue of George III which stood in New York City's Bowling Green Square. When the statue fell, so did a good many other English traditions and models that had long provided comfort and support for the colonial psyche. The pedestal that the King had shared with other popular and inspirational English heroes could not long stand bare in a new nation seeking some sort of stable identity. The citizenry needed somebody to believe in, to admire, to inspire, to use, even to abuse.

With the erection in 1792 of a statue of George Washington atop the same pedestal once occupied by the English king, the nation transferred its loyalties. Washington, never desirous but always accommodating, submitted himself to be "altogether at their beck, and sit like patience on a Monument." From that moment onward, Washington occupied a position never matched by any successor, a position of unequalled exposure that brought him everything from deification to contempt.

Figure 1
La Destruction de la Statue Royale a Nouvelle Yorck, hand-colored French engraving, late 18th century. The statue of George III, which stood on Bowling Green in New York City, was pulled down by American patriots in 1776 and melted to provide lead for bullets.
National Museum of American History.

Koniglichen Bild | La Destruction de la Statue royale

Neu Yorck   APuris chez Basset Rue St Jacques.   a Nouvelle Yorck

19

This Plate is with our RESPECT Inscribed to the CONGRESS of the United States, by

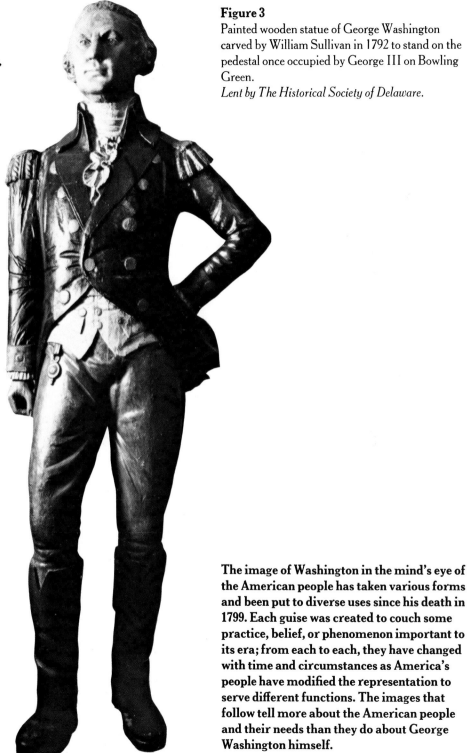

Figure 2
Engraving of the statue of George Washington on the pedestal at Bowling Green, drawn by Charles Buston, M.D., and engraved by Cornelius Tiebout, 1798.
National Museum of American History.

Figure 3
Painted wooden statue of George Washington carved by William Sullivan in 1792 to stand on the pedestal once occupied by George III on Bowling Green.
Lent by The Historical Society of Delaware.

The image of Washington in the mind's eye of the American people has taken various forms and been put to diverse uses since his death in 1799. Each guise was created to couch some practice, belief, or phenomenon important to its era; from each to each, they have changed with time and circumstances as America's people have modified the representation to serve different functions. The images that follow tell more about the American people and their needs than they do about George Washington himself.

CELEBRATED

Washington atop his national pedestal served as a pretext for a succession of national celebrations. A splendid series of spectacular entertainments marking great events and commemorating anniversaries swirled and sounded about him. Celebrations associated with George Washington during his lifetime ranged from processions after battle victories to annual birthday balls. Some of the most elaborate festivities marked his inauguration as President.

Figure 4
Salute to General Washington in New York Harbor, on the occasion of his inauguration, by L.M. Cooke, last quarter 19th century.
Oil on canvas, 27″ × 40¼″.
National Gallery of Art; gift of Edgar William and Bernice Chrysler Garbisch.

Figure 5
Engraving of Washington, inscribed
WASHINGTON, mounted on the back of a
pocket mirror.
From the Ralph E. Becker Collection,
National Museum of American History.

Figure 6
Sheet music of *Hail Columbia or the President's*
March as Performed at the Principle Theatres
Throughout the United States, composed to
celebrate the inauguration.
From the Ralph E. Becker Collection,
National Museum of American History.

The exhibition also includes:

America Presenting at the Altar of Liberty Medallions
of her Illustrious Sons, English plate-printed cotton
yard goods, c.1785.
National Museum of American History.

Clothing buttons made to be worn by spectators
at Washington's inauguration.
National Museum of American History.

Broadside with the words to *Hail Columbia*
distributed to the public, c.1789.
From the Ralph E. Becker Collection,
National Museum of American History.

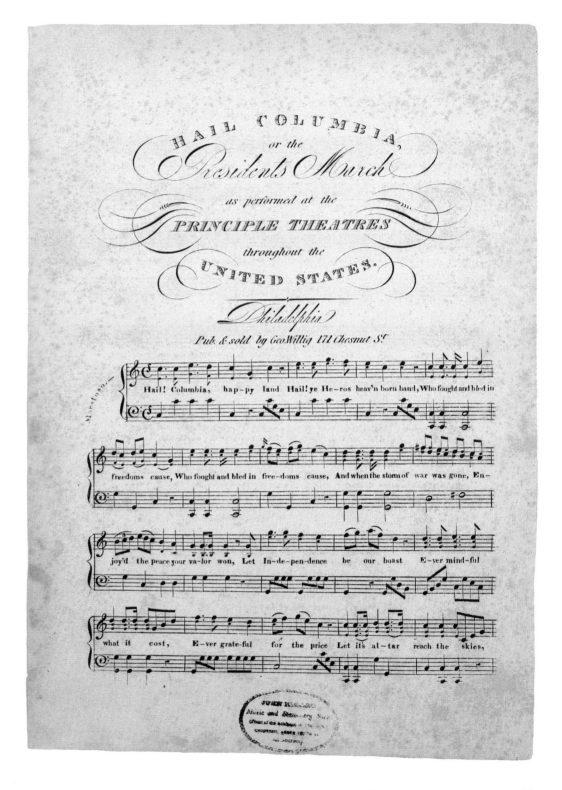

Widespread celebrations marked the centennial anniversary of George Washington's birth, February 22, 1832.

Figure 7
Gloria Patria.
National Museum of American History.

The exhibition also includes:

Printed ribbons worn by celebrants: *Centennial, He Still Lives in the Hearts of his Countrymen,* and *Centennial Anniversary.*
National Museum of American History.

Silk Masonic apron made to commemorate George Washington's 100th birthday.
Lent by the Daughters of the American Revolution Museum; gift of Mrs. Mary R. Moore and Mrs. Pleasant B. Meyers.

Medal *Struck & Distributed in Civic Procession Febry 22nd 1832 the Centennial Anniversary of the Birth Day of Washington by the Gold & Silver Artificers of Philad.*
National Museum of American History.

Figure 8
Lady Washington, a fire pumper built by James Smith in 1832 for the Martha Washington Fire Company in New York City. A painted panel shows Liberty bestowing upon a bust of George Washington a crown of thirteen stars. *Lent by The Adirondack Museum.*

Celebrations marking the centennial of American Independence in 1876 often featured George Washington.

Figure 10
Top of cotton patchwork quilt made in Charleston, New Hampshire, from souvenir textiles printed in 1876. Bottom of quilt appears on page 30.
National Museum of American History.

Figure 9
Tin belt buckle with miniature likenesses of George and Martha Washington, *1776/1876.*
From the Ralph E. Becker Collection,
National Museum of American History.

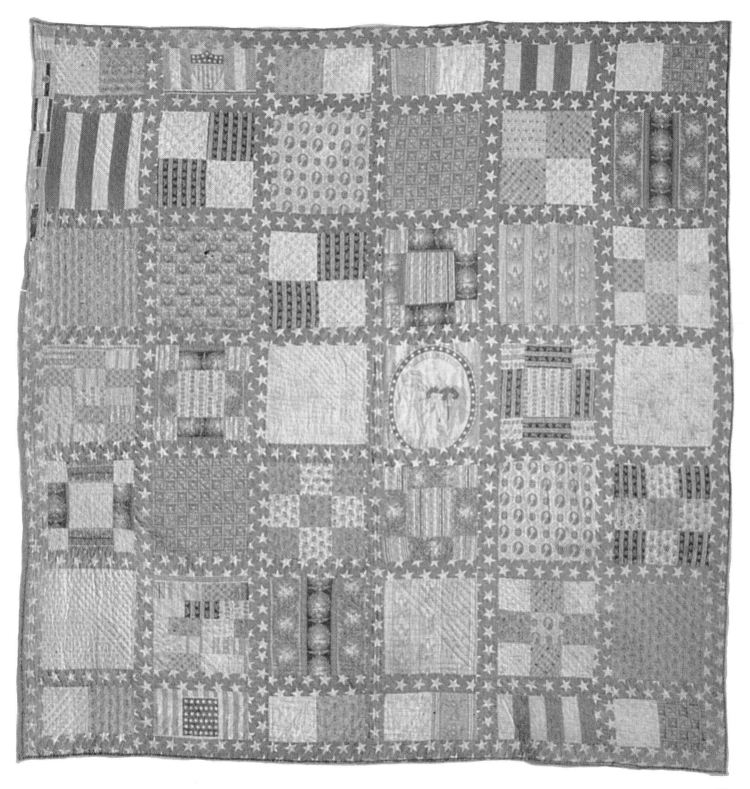

29

The exhibition also includes:

Woven jacquard with portrait of George Washington and scenes from the fairgrounds, a *memento/souvenir* of the International Exhibition at Philadelphia in 1876.
National Museum of American History.

Woven ribbons from the Centennial Exhibition bearing portraits of George Washington and the legends:
Centennial/1776-1876/Philadelphia/USA;
Centennial/USA/The Father of Our Country;
The Father of His Country; and
In Commemoration of the Centennial of American Independence.
National Museum of American History.

Paper lantern with likeness of George Washington.
National Museum of American History.

Photographic likeness of George Washington in a rosette of red, white, and blue ribbon.
National Museum of American History.

Silver medal honoring George Washington, struck for the Philadelphia Exhibition by Denmark, 1876.
National Museum of American History.

Silver medal *struck to perpetuate the memory of Washington,* 1876.
National Museum of American History.

Wooden souvenir medallion with profile of George Washington, 1876.
From the Ralph E. Becker Collection,
National Museum of American History.

Frosted glass souvenir plate with a relief bust of George Washington, 1876.
National Museum of American History.

Printed cotton banner depicting General Washington beside his horse on a field of red and white stripes, English, 1876.
National Museum of American History.

Hand-painted cotton banner with portrait of George Washington.
National Museum of American History.

Sketch Washington Monument & Grounds
24 Schd 1850   M C Meigs

32

Wash. Monument 24 Sept '50

The Continental Congress considered building a memorial to George Washington as early as 1783. It wasn't until the middle of the next century, however, and through the efforts of private citizens, that work actually began on a national monument. The construction of the monument was marked by patriotic rallying, dignified ceremonies, and festive jubilation.

Figure 11
Sketch of the Washington monument under construction, by Montgomery C. Meigs, September 22, 1850.
National Museum of American History.

The exhibition also includes:

Medal commemorating the laying of the cornerstone for the *National Monument* to Washington, July 4, 1848. The proposed design for the Washington monument, by Robert Mills, called for a 600-foot obelisk surrounded by a circular colonnade containing a huge statue of Washington and smaller ones of later Presidents and other notable Americans.
From the Ralph E. Becker Collection, National Museum of American History.

Certificate of Membership in the Washington National Monument Society, conferred upon Norman N. Hill for his contribution of one dollar *in aid of the erection of the Washington National Monument,* 1850. The Monument Society, organized in 1833 to build a shrine to Washington, raised money through popular subscription.
National Museum of American History.

Receipt to Augustine Harman for his contribution of one dollar to the erection of *the loftiest monument on earth to a nation's greatest benefactor,* January 2, 1852. The fund drive was *earnestly recommended* by such notables as John Quincy Adams, Henry Clay, President Millard Fillmore, and Daniel Webster.
National Museum of American History.

Figure 12
Box to collect contributions for *the National Monument to Washington*, which was *still unfinished* in 1853. Political squabbling, a lag in fund raising, and growing sectional antagonism brought construction to a halt a year later.
National Museum of American History.

The exhibition also includes:

Receipt to Daniel J. Turner for his contribution of two dollars.
Lent by Herbert R. Collins.

Medal depicting the uncompleted monument, 1875. Satirizing the popular accolade, it pronounced George Washington *First in War, First in Peace, Last in Securing a Monument.* A year later, President Grant approved legislation empowering the Federal Government to assume responsibility for completing the monument. Construction was resumed in 1880.
From the Ralph E. Becker Collection, National Museum of American History.

Invitation to the *Ceremonies on the completion of the Washington Monument,* February 21, 1885.
National Museum of American History.

Ticket admitting the bearer *to seat on platform* for the ceremony dedicating the Washington Monument.
National Museum of American History.

Order of Proceedings Adopted by the Congressional Commission for the Dedication of the Washington Monument February 21, 1885.
National Museum of American History.

Ribbon of the *Congressional Commission for the Dedication.*
National Museum of American History.

Monument Chart, a lithograph celebrating the height of the completed Washington Monument.
National Museum of American History.

Souvenir badge depicting the Washington Monument.
From the Ralph E. Becker Collection, National Museum of American History.

Figure 13
The Daily Graphic, February 23, 1885, showing fireworks at the base of the Monument on the evening of the dedication *from sketches by our special artist.*
National Museum of American History.

The centennial anniversary of the first inauguration of George Washington in April of 1889 was marked by celebrations around the country. The official celebration was held in New York City, where Washington had taken the oath of office in 1789.

Figure 14
Silver envelope and invitations sent to President Benjamin Harrison, who was the guest of honor at the official Inaugural Centennial celebration in New York City.
National Museum of American History.

Figure 15
Judge magazine, April 22, 1889. *A Big Boy's Welcome* shows Uncle Sam greeting George and Martha Washington on the occasion of the centennial of Washington's first inauguration.
From the Ralph E. Becker Collection, National Museum of American History.

VOL. 16 NO. 393   APRIL 27 1889.   PRICE 10 CENTS.

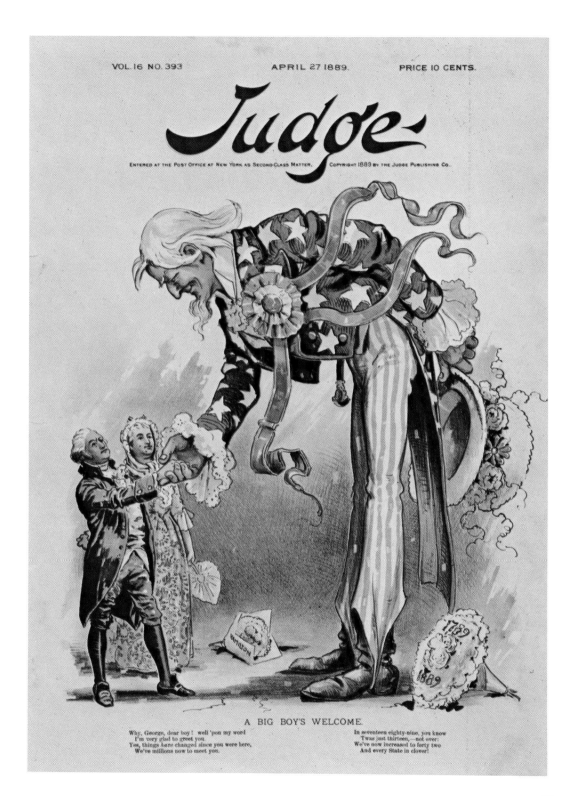

ENTERED AT THE POST OFFICE AT NEW YORK AS SECOND-CLASS MATTER.   COPYRIGHT 1889 BY THE JUDGE PUBLISHING CO.

A BIG BOY'S WELCOME.

Why, George, dear boy! well 'pon my word
    I'm very glad to greet you.
Yes, things have changed since you were here,
    We've millions now to meet you.

In seventeen eighty-nine, you know
    'Twas just thirteen,—not over:
We've now increased to forty two
    And every State in clover!

Figure 16
Street Dec[oration] and *Fireworks*,
badges and ribbons identifying official participants
in the 1889 centennial activities.
From the Ralph E. Becker Collection,
National Museum of American History.

The exhibition also includes:

Badge from the 1889 celebration:
Soldiers Medal/Participated.
From the Ralph E. Becker Collection,
National Museum of American History.

Souvenir ribbons and badges from the 1889
festivities:
Centennial Inauguration,
Washington/Harrison, 1789-1889,
an eagle with shield,
George Washington, First President,
and a 42-star flag.
From the Ralph E. Becker Collection,
National Museum of American History.

Guest badge for the celebration in New York,
modeled after a special medal designed by Augustus
St. Gaudens and struck to mark the occasion.
Badges of this style were worn by official dignitaries
and their guests.
National Museum of American History.

Program of ceremonies, 1889. The celebration in
New York City included a Wall Street parade, a
banquet, a ball, religious services, a military parade,
a concert at Madison Square, fireworks, a civic and
industrial parade, and an exhibition of relics.
National Museum of American History.

Program for a *Banquet at the Metropolitan Opera
House Given in honor of the Centennial of the
Inauguration,* April 20, 1889.
National Museum of American History.

Ticket for the Centennial Ball, held *Monday
Evening, April 29, 1889.*
National Museum of American History.

Ticket for the *Civic and Industrial Parade,*
May 1, 1889.
National Museum of American History.

Ticket for the *Loan Exhibition of Historical
Portraits and Relics.*
National Museum of American History.

The History of the Centennial Celebration of the Inauguration of George Washington as First President of the United States, edited by Clarence Winthrop Bowen, Secretary of the Committee, 1892.
National Museum of American History.

Ceramic souvenir mug decorated with portraits of Presidents George Washington and Benjamin Harrison.
National Museum of American History.

ABC (alphabet) plate with portrait of George Washington, sold as a commemorative souvenir in 1889.
National Museum of American History.

Souvenir medals inscribed:
Souvenir of the Centennial Festival;
Where he was Inaugurated First President;
George Washington, 1789;
First President of the United States of America;
and *George Washington.*
From the Ralph E. Becker Collection,
National Museum of American History.

Figure 17
Cast iron hatchet made as a souvenir to commemorate the inauguration of George Washington as President, 1889.
National Museum of American History.

The bicentennial anniversary of the birth of George Washington in 1932 was marked by an elaborate nationwide celebration masterminded by the Hon. Sol Bloom, a Congressman. A national commission established by Congress sought to include all Americans in a full year of activities in "every state, city, town and community."

Figure 18
Map of the Principal Events in the Life of George Washington, distributed by the Standard Oil Company of New Jersey during the 1932 bicentennial celebration, encouraging all Americans to *make this a Washington year*.
National Museum of American History.

MAKE THIS A WASHINGTON YEAR

This year the people of the United States celebrate the 200th anniversary of the birth of George Washington.

The celebrations which will be held throughout the country during 1932 add special interest to the hundreds of places associated with the name and life of Washington.

As an aid to you in taking your part in these celebrations and as a guide to Washington's historic shrines in the East and South we have prepared this special map showing the location of his principal activities, in peace and in war, from the Hudson to Savannah.

This year your family and your guests will be more interested than ever before in visiting the shrines of our country's first President. May we suggest therefore that you will enjoy including at least one of these historic places every time you take an automobile trip. Make this a Washington year.

STANDARD OIL COMPANY OF NEW JERSEY

Washington as a Surveyor

MAP
of the
Principal Events
in the life of
GEORGE WASHINGTON

contributed to the
Bicentennial Celebration
of his birth
by the

STANDARD OIL COMPANY OF NEW JERSEY

EXITUS ACTA PROBAT

Washington at Valley Forge

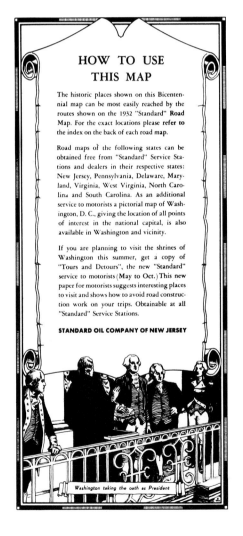

HOW TO USE THIS MAP

The historic places shown on this Bicentennial map can be most easily reached by the routes shown on the 1932 "Standard" Road Map. For the exact locations please **refer to** the index on the back of each road map.

Road maps of the following states can be obtained free from "Standard" Service Stations and dealers in their respective states: New Jersey, Pennsylvania, Delaware, Maryland, Virginia, West Virginia, North Carolina and South Carolina. As an additional service to motorists a pictorial map of Washington, D. C., giving the location of all points of interest in the national capital, is also available in Washington and vicinity.

If you are planning to visit the shrines of Washington this summer, get a copy of "Tours and Detours", the new "Standard" service to motorists (May to Oct.) This new paper for motorists suggests interesting places to visit and shows how to avoid road construction work on your trips. Obtainable at all "Standard" Service Stations.

STANDARD OIL COMPANY OF NEW JERSEY

Washington taking the oath as President

Figure 19
Flag used to decorate during the bicentennial celebration.
National Museum of American History.

The exhibition also includes:

Printed cotton bunting from the 1932 festivities.
National Museum of American History.

Itinerary and ticket for a special pilgrimage made by the General Assembly of Virginia to Wakefield and Alexandria to mark the 1932 bicentennial.
National Museum of American History.

Cast bronze statue of Washington, copied by the Gorham Company in 1932 from the original by Jean Antoine Houdon in the State Capitol at Richmond, Virginia, by special permission of the General Assembly of Virginia.
Lent by The George Washington University Permanent Collection, The Dimock Gallery.

Ribbon marking the *Pilgrimage to Wakefield, Fredericksburg, Alexandria and Mount Vernon,* worn by members of the General Assembly of Virginia.
National Museum of American History.

Postcards sold at the site of the 1730s-style colonial mansion reconstructed by the National Park Service at Wakefield, Virginia, to celebrate the bicentennial of Washington's birth, 1932. Interior views included the east bedchamber, kitchen, dining room, and drawing room.
Lent by Stephen William Cooper Holbrook.

Souvenir pins, badges, and buttons worn by celebrants across the nation, proclaiming:
Washington Bicentennial;
George Washington Bicentennial;
200th Anniversary 1732/1932;
Washington Bicentennial 1732-1932/Official Profile;
George Washington Bicentennial; and
Bicentennial/1732-1932/George Washington.
National Museum of American History.

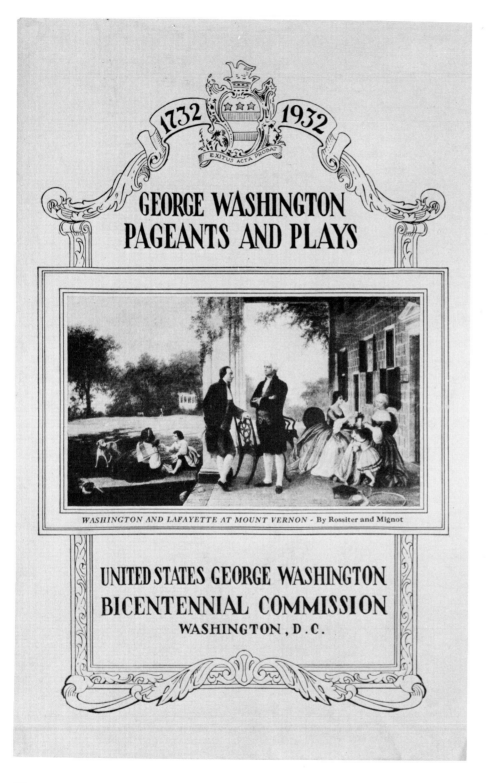

Figure 20
George Washington Pagents and Plays depicting the Life of George Washington and His Times, a booklet produced by the U.S. George Washington Bicentennial Commission for use by *educational, patriotic, religious, social, civic, fraternal and dramatic organizations* during the *nation-wide celebration.* *National Museum of American History.*

Figure 21
Boy's *Costume for George Washington
Bi-Centennial/Style: George Washington
President.*
National Museum of American History.

AT WORK ON HIS WASHINGTON ESSAY . . . . THIS COVER DESIGN, PAINTED FOR SEARS, ROEBUCK AND CO. BY NORMAN ROCKWELL, HAS BEEN APPROVED BY THE GEORGE WASHINGTON BICENTENNIAL COMMISSION . . . . SEE PAGE 87

SEARS, ROEBUCK AND CO.
CHICAGO

Figure 22

Sears, Roebuck and Co. catalog featuring
Guiding Influence, the Norman Rockwell
painting of a schoolboy *at work on his
Washington Essay*, 1932. A special inside page
publicized the planned nationwide activities
and offered for sale a variety of bicentennial
souvenirs.
Lent by Sears, Roebuck and Co.

The exhibition also includes:

Ribbon with portrait of George Washington
on a flag background used for the 1932
bicentennial celebration of his birth.
National Museum of American History.

Medallion bearing the *official profile* of the
1932 celebration.
*From the Ralph E. Becker Collection,
National Museum of American History.*

Bicentennial medals with the *official profile* on
the obverse and Washington's Birthplace on
the reverse.
National Museum of American History.

Silver quarter-dollar coin with the official
profile of George Washington on the obverse,
issed by an Act of Congress in 1932.
National Museum of American History.

Girl's costume for bicentennial pagents and
plays, an *approved* design produced by
George Washington Bicentennial Costumes,
New York.
National Museum of American History.

Sheet music of *Father of the Land We Love*,
composed by George M. Cohan for the 1932
celebration.
National Museum of American History.

Program for a service held in New York by
the National Council of the Protestant
Episcopal Church in honor of the
bicentennial.
National Museum of American History.

Guiding Influence, by Norman Rockwell,
c.1932.
Oil on canvas, $38'' \times 28\frac{1}{2}''$.
This painting was commissioned as part of
the campaign to inspire students of public
schools in an essay contest sponsored by the
Bicentennial Commission. More than
5,000,000 posters of this design were
distributed to classrooms around the nation.
Lent by Jack D. Parker.

Official commemorative bronze medal,
designed by Laura Gardin Fraser. Struck in
gold, silver, and bronze, these medals were
awarded to winners in national and state
declamatory, essay, and oratorical contests.
National Museum of American History.

Crocheted bedspread commemorating the
bicentennial, 1932.
National Museum of American History.

Frosted glass souvenir plate with bust of
George Washington, 1932.
National Museum of American History.

Queensware ceramic souvenir plate with
transfer portrait of George Washington, 1932.
National Museum of American History.

Amber glass souvenir vase decorated with
medallion portrait of George Washington,
1932.
National Museum of American History.

Glass souvenir flask with side view portrait of
George Washington, 1932.
National Museum of American History.

Commemorative envelope, *Washington
Bicentennial 1932*.
*From the Ralph E. Becker Collection,
National Museum of American History.*

George Washington Memorial Parkway
entrance sign. The bicentennial celebration
in 1932 inspired the construction of a
parkway which eventually extended along
the Potomac River from south of Great Falls
to Mount Vernon.
Lent by the U.S. National Park Service.

Cotton kerchief designed by Mildred G.
Burrage and printed by F. Schumacher, 1933.
These kerchiefs were sold for a dollar each to
raise money for the construction of the
George Washington Parkway.
National Museum of American History.

Even without great events or anniversaries to mark, the American people delighted in George Washington.

Figure 23
Celebration of Washington's Birthday at Malta on Board U.S.S. Constitution, *Commodore Jesse D. Elliot, by James G. Evans, 1837. Oil on canvas, 26" × 38". Lent by the U.S. Naval Academy Museum.*

Celebration of

The exhibition also includes:

Colored etchings of *General and Lady Washington* published by J. Testi, 10 Leather Lane, London, c.1810. As the etcher had no portrait of Martha to follow, he slightly modified a likeness of Josephine Bonaparte to represent Martha Washington. *National Museum of American History.*

Transfer-printed Staffordshire enamel mirror knob with portrait of George Washington, early 19th century. *National Museum of American History.*

French ormolu bust of George Washington on a marbelite pedestal, c.1810. *Lent by The White House.*

Wreaths for the Chieftain, performed in Boston *at the celebration of Peace with Great Britain and the Birth Day of Genl. Washington, Feb. 22nd, 1815.* The tune is an early version of *Hail to the Chief. National Museum of American History.*

Figurehead of the USS *Washington*, a painted wooden bust of George Washington carved by Solomon Willard in 1816 for the ship built at Portsmouth, New Hampshire, in 1815. *Lent by the U.S. Naval Academy Museum.*

Silk umbrella with a portrait of George Washington decorating the handle, c.1824. *National Museum of American History.*

Leather fire bucket with handpainted portrait of George Washington and the legend, *Veni, Vidi, Vici* (I came, I saw, I conquered), c.1830. *National Museum of American History.*

Polychrome ceramic bust of George Washington made by Enoch Wood, a Staffordshire potter, in England for export to the American market, early 19th century. *National Museum of American History.*

Redware bust of George Washington by an unknown Pennsylvania potter after the Enoch Wood design, mid-19th century. *National Museum of American History.*

Bronze statuette of George Washington in uniform by an unknown sculptor, mid-19th century. *Lent by The White House.*

hington' Birth Day at MALTA on board the U.S.S. CONSTITUTION. Comm. J.D.ELLIOT. 1837

47

Figure 24
The Grand "Washington Monument"
Procession, as it Appeared on Hamilton Square
During the Ceremony of Laying the Corner-
stone, October 19th, 1847, by
J. Baillie of New York.
Lithograph with watercolor.
National Museum of American History.

The exhibition also includes:

Ribbon in commemoration of laying the
cornerstone of the Washington Monument
in 1847.
National Museum of American History.

Design of a National Monument to be Erected
at Washington's Head Quarters at Newburgh,
N.Y., lithograph by John Pennimen after a
drawing by S.B. Brophy, published by
Endicott, mid-19th century.
Lent by The White House.

Washington Monument at Richmond, Virginia,
engraving by John Rogers, published by
Virtue & Co., New York, c.1850.
Lent by The White House.

LITH & PUB. BY J. BAILLIE,

THE G
As it appeared

O "WASHINGTON MONUMENT" PROCESSION;

ton Square during the Ceremony of laying the Corner-stone, October 19th 1847.

On Stone from a Drawing taken on the Spot by J.L.Magee

Figure 25
Washington Crossing the Delaware, by
Eastman Johnson, 1851, after Emanuel
Leutze.
Oil on canvas, $40\frac{1}{2}'' \times 68''$.
Lent from a private collection.

The exhibition also includes:

Straight razor with a figure of George
Washington and the legend *Washington/
Champion of Liberty* etched on the blade,
manufactured by Fred K. Reynolds,
Sheffield, England, mid-19th century.
National Museum of American History.

Scrimshawed whale tooth decorated with a
portrait of George Washington by *J. Hayden,
NY/Feb. 1861.*
*Lent by the Museum of the City of New York;
gift of Mrs. Screven Lorillard.*

Chair made from a branch of the *Washington
Elm*, under which—by tradition—George
Washington took command of the Continental
Army on the Common in Cambridge,
Massachusetts, mid-19th century.
National Museum of American History.

Center table decorated with a wood inlay of
George Washington, c.1875.
National Museum of American History.

Flag of the State of Washington bearing a
portrait of George Washington. Washington,
the forty-second state, was admitted to the
Union on November 11, 1889.
National Museum of American History.

Reproduction of the Washington Memorial
window made of stained glass by Maria
Herndl in 1901. The original window is
located in the Senators' private dining room,
United States Capitol.
*Courtesy of the Office of the Architect of
the Capitol.*

52

Figure 26
George Washington's Cherry Tree Quilt, made in Versailles, Kentucky, before 1852.
Lent by the Huntington Galleries.

Figure 27
Princess Beatrice, a tattooed lady on the circus and dime show circuit, adorned with a portrait of George Washington as shown in a photograph from the early 20th century.
Reproduced from America's Forgotten Folk Arts, *by Fred and Mary Fried.*

The exhibition also includes:

Ribbon from a Washington's Birthday celebration in Philadelphia, 1916.
National Museum of American History.

Bridge tally in the shape of a hatchet used for a party held on Washington's Birthday, 1930s.
National Museum of American History.

Pin with colored portrait of George Washington and red, white, and blue ribbons.
National Museum of American History.

State of Virginia automobile license plate bearing the profile of George Washington surrounded by stars, 1976.
National Museum of American History.

Silk necktie woven with scene of *Washington Crossing the Delaware*, and the American Bicentennial logo, 1976.
National Museum of American History.

Northern Virginia telephone directory showing detail from John Trumbull's painting *Surrender of Lord Cornwallis at Yorktown*, published by the Chesapeake and Potomac Telephone Company, 1981.
National Museum of American History.

Figure 28

I send you patriotic Greetings on his Birthday, a postcard decorated with a portrait of George Washington and a view of Mount Vernon. *National Museum of American History.*

Figure 29

Lace tablecloth with scene of *Washington Crossing the Delaware*, manufactured by the Quaker Lace Company, 1976. *National Museum of American History.*

SENTIMENTALIZED

Washington's position on the lofty national pedestal has frequently elicited what now seems to be a mawkish kind of adoration among many Americans. Particularly during the Victorian era, Washington was viewed with fond and uncritical affection; well into the 20th century he was held dear to many hearts. Images of his person and character are marked by effusive sweetness and goodness.

Figure 30

Heart-shaped box made from the wood of Washington's first coffin, after 1831.
Lent by the National Society of the Colonial Dames of America.

Figure 31

Eulogium Sacred to the Memory of the Illustrious George Washington, designed, written, and published by Benjamin O. Tyler, engraved by P. Maverick, 1815.
National Museum of American History.

The exhibition also includes:

Drawing of General George Washington on a rearing horse *executed with the pen by Benj P. Chadwick,* early 19th century.
Watercolor and ink.
National Museum of American History.

The Grave of Washington, Composed and Sung by Harmoneans, published by Oliver Ditson, Boston, 1846. *Disturb not his slumbers let Washington sleep . . . ,* read the lyrics, *Let him rest undisturbed on Potomac's far shore; On the rivers green border so flowery drest, with the hearts he loved fondly, let Washington rest. National Museum of American History.*

Piece of George Washington's cherry tree. By the middle of the 19th century, the cherry tree legend had become such a part of American mythology that people were cherishing "actual" pieces of the legendary tree. An accompanying affidavit affirms that *this piece of cherry wood came from a stump which, according to tradition, was left from the original cherry tree chopped down by our first president as a boy.*
Lent by the Wayside Inn Since 1797.

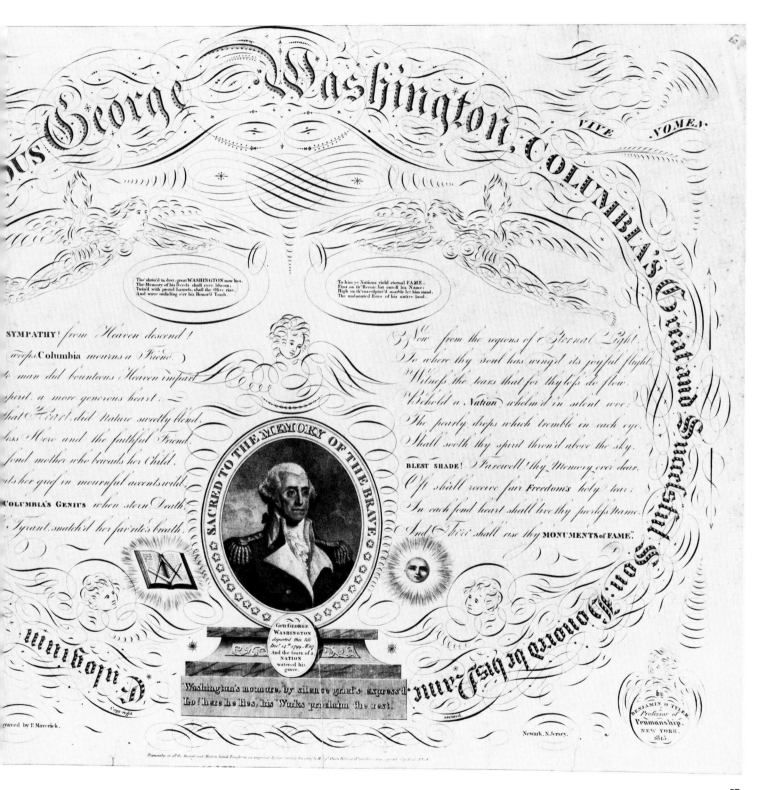

Wood cuts, engravings, and lithographs depicting George Washington were produced in abundance for mass-market sales. As one European visitor to America in the 19th century observed, "Every American considers it his sacred duty to have a likeness of Washington in his home, just as we have images of God's saints."

The exhibition also includes:

Popular prints reflecting the affection Americans
have felt for George Washington throughout
U.S. history:
Framed engraving of George Washington, published
by H.R. Hall's Sons, New York;
Washington in 1772, engraved by J.W. Steel, 1830;
Washington at Prayer, by E.G. and E.C. Kellogg,
c.1856;
Washington at Valley Forge, from *Harper's Weekly*,
1783; and
Washington's Farewell to the Army, by Berlin
Photographic Company, 1903.
National Museum of American History.

Ceramic dish with transfer print of George
Washington's tomb.
National Museum of American History.

Washington—His Kindness, a postcard depicting the
General feeding a sugar cube to his horse, early
20th century.
Lent by Howard A. Morrison.

George Washington doll of parian with stuffed
cloth body, made by Emma Clear of San Francisco,
1950.
Lent by the Perelman Antique Toy Museum.

Miniature of room in the Potts House, which
served as Washington's headquarters at Valley
Forge, made by E.J. Kupjack, c.1980.
Lent by E.J. Kupjack Associates, Inc.

Figure 34
Molds for making chocolate figures of
George Washington, late 19th century.
National Museum of American History.

61

DOMESTICATED

The years before the Civil War were a time of
flux marked by rapid technological progress,
accelerating territorial expansion, and
expanding areas of human exploit. Amidst
this swirl of change, the home and the family
were felt to constitute a haven of undisturbed
peace, security, and domestic tranquillity.
Washington, standing stable and unchanging
atop his pedestal, soon became identified with
the comfort of the fireside. As the cult of
domesticity was broadened to encompass the
country as a whole, Washington became the
strong Father for a national American Family,
and Mount Vernon became their national
Home.

Figure 35
Washington Family, lithograph by E.R. and
E.C. Kellogg, Hartford, Connecticut, c.1845.
National Museum of American History.

The exhibition also includes:

Washington and His Family, hand-colored engraving.
From the Ralph E. Becker Collection,
National Museum of American History.

Washington & Family, lithograph by Kellogg
& Bulkeley, Hartford, Connecticut, c.1860.
National Museum of American History.

Washington Family, lithograph by H. Schile and
Company, New York, 1869.
National Museum of American History.

Washington.   G. Washington.   Lady Washington.

WASHINGTON FAMILY.

E.B. & E.C. Kellogg 136 Main St. Hartford, Conn.   D. Needham 223. Main St. Buffalo.

Under the terms of George Washington's Will, Bushrod Washington, his nephew, came into possession of Mount Vernon. By the 1850s, however, the care of the Mansion had become too great a burden for the descendants to continue. Both the Federal Government and the State of Virginia declined to buy it. Miss Ann Pamela Cunningham of South Carolina spearheaded an appeal to the women of the United States to rescue the "hallowed spot," and in 1858 "The Mount Vernon Ladies' Association of the Union" purchased Washington's home "To forever hold, manage and preserve the estate, properties and relics . . . and to open the same to the inspection of all who love the cause of liberty and revere the name of Washington."

Figure 36
Certificate entitling William Roe to membership in the *Ladies' Mount Vernon Association of the Union . . . by virtue of a contribution of $20-dollars*, February 22, 1859.
National Museum of American History.

The exhibition also includes:

An Appeal to the Ladies of the State of Virginia for the Purchase of Mount Vernon, a circular soliciting funds for the purchase and preservation of the estate, c.1858.
Lent by the Mount Vernon Ladies' Association.

Subscription paper of the Mount Vernon Association of the Union, addressed to the Ladies of the Union, c.1858. *To you we now extend the highest privilege ever granted to American women, one which should thrill every fibre of our hearts as the daughters of one common "Father."* The paper invited women to join in the effort to *secure and hallow, through all coming time, the Home and Grave of the "Father of our country."*
Lent by the Mount Vernon Ladies' Association.

Mount Vernon and Its Associations, by Benson J. Lossing, published in New York by W.A. Townsend and Company, 1859. This book, dedicated to the *Patriotic Countrywomen by whose efforts the Home and Tomb of Washington have been rescued from decay*, helped to nurture continued public interest in Mount Vernon.
Lent by Herbert R. Collins.

Visit of the Members of Congress to the Tomb of Washington by Invitation From the Ladies of the Mount Vernon Association, Now Placed in Possession of the Estate, a print from *Harper's Weekly*, March 7, 1860. The Association hoped that *the guests might, from observation, testify to the country the need there is for the generous and patriotic* to contribute funds for the renovation of the estate.
From the Ralph E. Becker Collection, National Museum of American History.

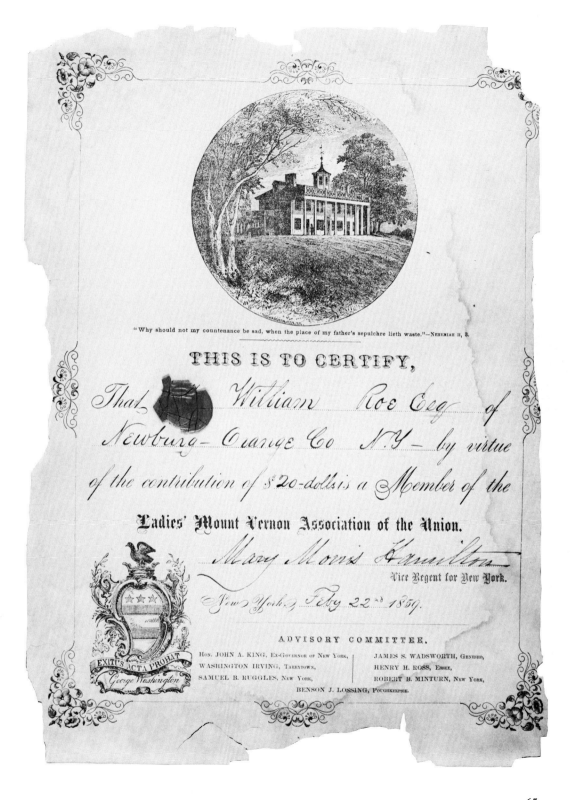

"Why should not my countenance be sad, when the place of my father's sepulchre lieth waste."—NEHEMIAH II, 3.

THIS IS TO CERTIFY,

That *William Roe Esq* of *Newburg Orange Co N.Y* by virtue of the contribution of $20 dollars a Member of the

Ladies' Mount Vernon Association of the Union.

Mary Morris Hamilton

Vice Regent for New York.

New York, Feby 22nd 1859.

ADVISORY COMMITTEE.

Hon. JOHN A. KING, Ex-Governor of New York,   JAMES S. WADSWORTH, Geneseo,

WASHINGTON IRVING, Tarrytown,   HENRY H. ROSS, Essex,

SAMUEL B. RUGGLES, New York,   ROBERT B. MINTURN, New York,

BENSON J. LOSSING, Poughkeepsie.

EXITUS ACTA PROBAT

George Washington

From Childs & Inmans Lith Press.

Mount Vernon.

T. Doughty Del. from a Drawing by H. Reinagle.

Philadelphia Pubᵈ by Childs & Inman, Corner of 5ᵗʰ & Walnut Streets. 1832.

Figure 37
Mount Vernon, by Childs and Inman, 1832.
National Museum of American History.

The exhibition also includes:

Visit of the Prince of Wales to the Tomb of Washington at Mount Vernon, October 1860, by Thomas Pritchard Rossiter, 1861.
Oil on canvas, $27\frac{1}{2}'' \times 54\frac{3}{8}''$.
Lent by the National Museum of American Art, from the Harriet Lane Johnston Collection.

Commemorative miniature framed with wood *grown at Mount Vernon*. Some of the money from the sale of *this beautiful gem* went to the Mount Vernon Ladies' Association.
National Museum of American History.

Medal depicting *Washington's Residence at Mount Vernon.*
National Museum of American History.

Nineteenth century wood cuts, engravings and lithographs of Mount Vernon:
Mount Vernon;
Mount Vernon: The Birthplace and Residence of George Washington on the Potomac, engraved *expressly for the* Christian Family Annual, c.1850;
Mount Vernon—The Home of Washington;
Mount Vernon—The Home of Washington, 1861;
and *Mount Vernon* from *Harper's Weekly*, February 28, 1874.
National Museum of American History.

Silver box with engraving of Mount Vernon, by Tiffany and Company, mid-19th century.
National Museum of American History.

Cast iron ornamental figure of George Washington, patented in 1843 by Alonzo Blanchard. Such figures were often used to decorate cast iron heating stoves.
National Museum of American History.

Cast iron andirons in the figure of George Washington, of American manufacture, probably 19th century.
National Museum of American History.

Ornamental design for a furniture support incorporating a bust of George Washington, patented by James Fay of New York, June 30, 1903.
Reproduced by courtesy of the U.S. Patent Office.

Cast iron still bank in the figure of George Washington, c.1920.
Lent by the Perelman Antique Toy Museum.

George Washington's Crazy Quilt, by Sante Graziani, 1974.
Acrylic on canvas, $48'' \times 36''$.
Lent by the Babcock Galleries.

Figure 38
Covered vegetable dish with transfer print of
Mount Vernon Near Washington, one of the
Beauties of America series produced in Staffordshire
pottery by J.&W.Ridgway, c.1820.
National Museum of American History.

Figure 39
Cast iron ten-plate heating stove decorated with
a likeness of George Washington, made by the
Elizabeth Furnace, Lancaster County,
Pennsylvania, early 19th century.
Lent by the Edison Institute.

EXPLOITED

Americans could not long resist the temptation to identify themselves with the Washington on the pedestal; many scrambled to stand beside him in order to take advantage of the high regard and wide attention his image elicited. Washington became currency, to be used by a wide gamut of individuals and groups to sell products, politicians, and ideas.

Figure 40
Wooden sign for the *Temperance House* with a hand-painted depiction of General Washington standing beside a horse, 19th century.
National Museum of American History.

The exhibition also includes:

Ribbon decorated with tobacco plants and products issued by the Tobacconists of Philadelphia in commemoration of the centennial anniversary of George Washington's birth, 1832.
National Museum of American History.

Token distributed by T. Brimelow, Druggist, bearing the likeness of *Geo. Washington President*, 1863.
From the Ralph E. Becker Collection, National Museum of American History.

Linen sack for *Pure English Salt* manufactured by Stubbs Brothers, Cheshire, England, late 19th century. The stamp of the factory bears the likeness and name of Washington.
National Museum of American History.

Ceramic mug advertising the Washington Brewery Company, Washington, D.C.
From the Ralph E. Becker Collection, National Museum of American History.

Advertising broadside for Washington Mills, Gloucester, New Jersey, manufacturers of *American Cotton and Woolen Goods.*
National Museum of American History.

Set of four jugs in the figure of George Washington, American, c.1890.
National Museum of American History.

HAD WASHINGTON LIVED IN THESE DAYS
HE'D SAY WITH ALL THE REST
"I CANNOT, WILL NOT TELL A LIE,
DUKE'S DURHAM IS THE BEST."

THE YOUTHFUL WASHINGTON

A FEW TRUTHS

Figure 42
Gift tag depicting the cherry tree legend;
20th century.
National Museum of American History.

Figure 41
Trade cards exploiting the cherry tree legend,
20th century:
I Cannot Tell a Lie, Duke's Durham is the Best;
The Youthful Washington;
A Few Truths; and
Father I Cannot Tell a Lie.
National Museum of American History.

Figure 43

Tin container for George Washington Greatest American Cut Plug bearing a portrait of Washington, sold by R.J. Reynolds Tobacco Company, early 20th century.
Lent by William L. Bird Jr.

Figure 44

Poster advertising country music station WPKX-WVKX, Alexandria, Virginia, picturing George Washington wearing a cowboy hat, 1981.
National Museum of American History; gift of the artist, Jack Pardue.

The exhibition also includes:

Trade cards from the 20th century featuring George Washington as part of the promotion of a variety of products:
Between the Acts and Bravo Cigarettes; "Sweet Home" Soap; Try Van De Carr's Lovely Coffee; Compliments of Wood & Hall: Furniture, Carpets, Stoves and Undertaking; and *Washington Fire and Marine Insurance Company. National Museum of American History.*

Calligraphic novelty presenting the Declaration of Independence in the form of a bust of George Washington, distributed by Chambers and Son, General Agents of the Washington Life Insurance Company of New York, 19th century.
National Museum of American History.

Receipt from the George Washington Bank, Corning, New York.
National Museum of American History.

Pin with colored portrait of George Washington advertising *Cherry Smash*, a soft drink.
National Museum of American History.

Luncheon service with medallion portrait of George Washington, made by the Buffalo China Company for use aboard the *George Washington*, a train on the Chesapeake and Ohio Railroad, c.1932.
National Museum of American History.

Lapel pin with portrait of George Washington, distributed to advertise Sweet Corporal cigarettes, 1896.
From the Ralph E. Becker Collection, National Museum of American History.

The exhibition also includes:

Package of George Washington Great American
Pipe Tobacco produced by the R.J. Reynolds
Tobacco Company, 1980.
National Museum of American History.

Mount Vernon *in Pearls*, a model presented to the
United States by Kokichi Mikimoto, founder of the
cultured pearl industry in Japan, for display at the
Chicago World's Fair, 1933.
National Museum of American History.

Sunshine biscuit (cookie) tin with portrait of George
Washington and scenes from his life, produced by
the Loose-Wiles Biscuit Company, 1939.
Lent by Eleanor L. Boyne.

Illuminated sign from the General Washington Inn,
Fredericksburg, Virginia.
Lent by the General Washington Inn.

The Truth About George Washington's False Teeth,
a magazine advertisement produced by the Rhode
Island Tourist Promotion Division, 1980.
*Courtesy of Department of Economic Development,
State of Rhode Island and Providence Plantations.*

For the best father in the land . . . an advertisement
for Kodel fiber underwear which appeared in the
June 1980 issue of *Good Housekeeping* magazine.
Courtesy of Eastman Chemical Products.

The Father of Our Company, an advertisement for
the Washington Bank of Washington, D.C.
Courtesy of the Washington Bank.

Promotional brochure for Washington, England, an
industrial and residential community being
developed on the site of the ancestral home of the
Washington family by the Washington New Town
Development Corporation.
From Washington New Town Development Corporation.

T-shirt promoting Georgetown in
Washington, D.C., 1981.
Lent by Carolyn P. Davies.

Figure 45
Medal of the Washington Benevolent Society, 1808.
Members of the Whig Party sought their own
political aggrandisement by forming themselves into
this patriotic society which identified itself with
Washington as *defender of his country.*
National Museum of American History.

The exhibition also includes:

Ribbon of the Washington Benevolent Society for
the County of Columbia.
National Museum of American History.

*The Constitution of the Washington Benevolent
Society . . . to which are added the Farewell Address
of George Washington and the Constitutions of the
United States and the State of New York*, a booklet
published by Webster and Skinners, Albany,
New York, for members of the Society, 1814.
National Museum of American History.

*Order of Performances of the Third Publick
Celebration of the Washington Benevolent Society of
Massachusetts*, April 20, 1814.
National Museum of American History.

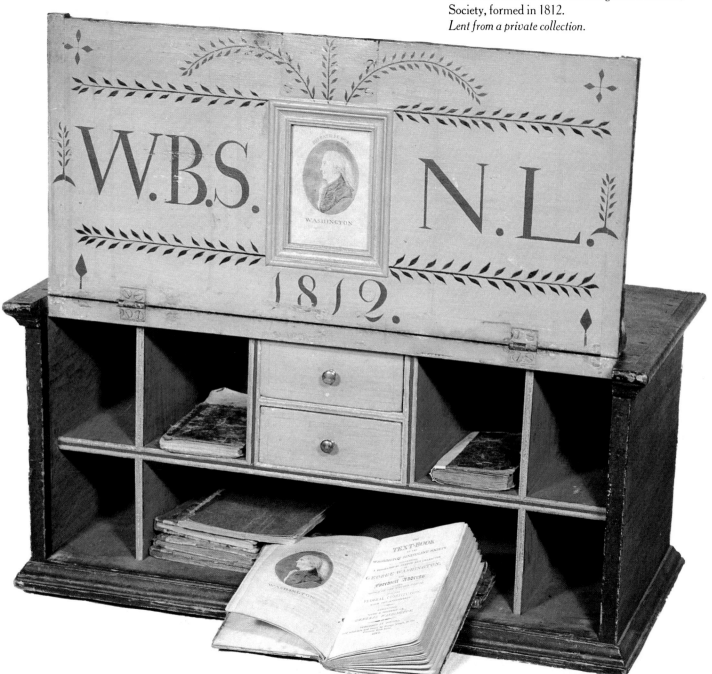

Figure 46
Painted wooden letter box with inscription
W.B.S./N.L./1812, probably used by secretary of
the Boston branch of the Washington Benevolent
Society, formed in 1812.
Lent from a private collection.

WHIG CELEBRATION
November 22d
1837
Glorious Triumph
of
JUST PRINCIPLES

THE SPIRIT OF
76
REVIVED IN 1837

Edward T Whalee N York Hand Co.

Figure 47
Whig Celebration ribbon, 1837.
From the Ralph E. Becker Collection,
National Museum of American History.

Figure 48
Bandanna identifying Abraham Lincoln, *The Savior of His Country*, with George Washington, *The Father of His Country*, probably produced for the 1860 election. Lincoln ran against Stephen A. Douglas, John Bell, and John C. Breckenridge.
National Museum of American History.

The exhibition also includes:

Political token with bust of Andrew Jackson on the obverse and George Washington on the reverse.
National Museum of American History.

Blown glass flask with profiles of Andrew Jackson and George Washington.
National Museum of American History.

Ribbon promoting the candidacy of William Henry Harrison during the presidential campaign of 1840. George Washington and Harrison were, according to its legend: *First in War—First in Peace—First in the Hearts of their Countrymen.*
National Museum of American History.

Banner for the presidential campaign of Henry Clay and Theodore Frelinghuysen in 1844. The reverse bears a portrait of George Washington and the legend, *The Whigs of Old Washington Will Stand by the Union.*
National Museum of American History.

Campaign lithograph of Henry Clay holding George Washington's *Liberty Cap* cane, 1844.
National Museum of American History.

Blown glass flask with a bust of George Washington (*The Father of His Country*) and a bust of Zachary Taylor (*Gen. Taylor Never Surrenders*) from the 1844 campaign.
From the Ralph E. Becker Collection,
National Museum of American History.

CENTENNIAL

THOMAS A. HENDRICKS — SAM⁰ J. TILDEN

DEMOCRATIC CANDIDATES FOR 1876.

Figure 49
Political campaign kerchief from the 1876 presidential campaign bearing portraits of George Washington and Democratic candidates Thomas A. Hendricks and Samuel J. Tilden.
National Museum of American History.

The exhibition also includes:

Electoral ticket for John Bell, nominated by the Constitutional Union Party in 1860. The graphic on the ticket is a bust portrait of Washington surrounded by a laurel wreath with the legend, *The Union, the Constitution and the Enforcement of the Laws.*
National Museum of American History.

Electoral ticket for presidential hopeful John C. Breckenridge, nominated by the Southern branch of the Democratic Party in 1860. The ticket is decorated with a portrait of George Washington and an appeal for *The Constitution, the Sovereignty and Equality of the States, and the Repeal of the Missouri Restriction . . . .*
From the Ralph E. Becker Collection, National Museum of American History.

Colored lithograph, tri-view campaign novelty of General George Washington, General Winfield Scott, and General George B. McClellan, who was running for president in 1864, made from prints by Currier & Ives.
Lent by the Edison Institute.

1889 to 1789 The Progress of Time, a political cartoon from *Judge* magazine. Politicians of 1889 are depicted speaking to George Washington: *Say, George, you couldn't make your living now. Why, you had no "gang," you didn't work for "Boodle," you were in no "deals" and you didn't even tell a lie.*
From the Ralph E. Becker Collection, National Museum of American History.

Washington Harrison Crossing the Delaware, a cartoon from *Judge* magazine parodying *a popular picture*, 1889. Benjamin Harrison, standing in a boat propelled across the river by members of his administration, encounters *office seekers* and *spoils grabbers*, who appear as blocks of ice in the water.
From the Ralph E. Becker Collection, National Museum of American History.

Political campaign badge from 1896 presidential campaign. A button decorated with portraits of Republican nominees William J. McKinley and Garret A. Hobart is suspended by a ribbon bearing a quotation from George Washington.
National Museum of American History.

The Washington-Bryan Combination Picture, a campaign novelty used in the 1896 presidential race to promote Democratic candidate William Jennings Bryan.
From the Ralph E. Becker Collection, National Museum of American History.

Reproduction of a campaign poster from the 1912 presidential race promoting Democratic candidate Woodrow Wilson: *I think We've Got Another Washington and Wilson is His Name.*
From the Ralph E. Becker Collection, National Museum of American History.

Certificate of appointment and official badge for an assistant Sergeant at Arms at the 1932 Republican National Convention. Both bear a portrait of George Washington.
From the Ralph E. Becker Collection, National Museum of American History.

Pillars of the Republic, a campaign novelty from the 1948 election showing *Founder* George Washington, *Preserver* Abraham Lincoln and *Defender* Thomas E. Dewey.
National Museum of American History.

Figure 50
Washington-MacArthur combination picture campaign novelty used in the 1952 presidential race to promote America First Party nominee Douglas MacArthur. MacArthur claimed dedication to the preservation of the *Divine Heritage* of Washington.
From the Ralph E. Becker Collection,
National Museum of American History.

Figure 51
Let Washington Speak, a poster advocating Congressional Voting Rights for Washington, D.C., 1977.
National Museum of American History.

The exhibition also includes:

E.R.A. Now, a button on which a cartoon of George Washington endorses the Equal Rights Amendment, c.1979.
National Museum of American History.

Independence Declared 1776/The Union Must Be Preserved, lithograph by Joseph A. Arnold, 1839.
National Museum of American History.

American Republican Celebration ribbon with a portrait of George Washington and a warning to *Beware of Foreign Influence*, 1844.
National Museum of American History.

American Republican Procession Nov. 4th 1844, a ribbon marking a gathering of American nativists, bearing the legend *This is my own native land*.
National Museum of American History.

Let Washington Speak.

Congressional Voting Rights for D.C.

© 1977 SELF-DETERMINATION FOR DC 2030 M STREET NW WASHINGTON, DC 2   J2183 3-1200

Figure 52
Ribbon celebrating the Fourth of July, 1865, and the memories of George Washington and Abraham Lincoln. A pin bears the bust of George Washington and the word *UNION*.
National Museum of American History.

Figure 53
For Old Glory, a sheet music supplement to the New York *Journal and Advertiser*, February 27, 1898. The Leutze depiction of Washington crossing the Delaware adorns the cover. *But we give solemn warning to the world as well as Spain, It means fight to insult the . . . flag that flew over Washington when liberty was won.*
National Museum of American History.

The exhibition also includes:

Envelopes promoting the Union, c. 1860: Washington and *UNION*, and Washington and *Long May Our Land Be Bright/With Freedom's Holy Light.*
From the Ralph E. Becker Collection,
National Museum of American History.

Medal with bust of Washington declaring *The Constitution is Sacredly Obligatory to All*, commemorating the oath of allegiance to the Union taken by the officers and workmen of the United States Mint, September 2, 1861.
National Museum of American History.

Medal with bust of George Washington which quotes from the Farewell Address, *Avoid the Extremes of Party Spirit.*
National Museum of American History.

Token with equestrian statue of George Washington and the legend *Union For Ever*, 1863.
From the Ralph E. Becker Collection,
National Museum of American History.

Medal with bust of George Washington quoting from a letter to Alexander Hamilton, *I hope that liberal allowances will be made for the political opinions of each other*, 1864.
National Museum of American History.

Medal with bust and the legend *George Washington/Security.*
National Museum of American History.

Figure 54
News photo of a 1939 rally of the German-American Bund at Madison Square Garden. Adorning the stage is a 30-foot banner with the likeness of George Washington flanked by stars and stripes and Nazi swastikas.
Courtesy of Photoworld, a Division of Freelance Photographers Guild Inc.

Figure 55
One Nation Under God, a poster used at a *Washington for Jesus* religious rally held on the Mall in Washington, D.C., in April 1980, depicting the statue of George Washington in prayer that was the symbol of the rally.
National Museum of American History.

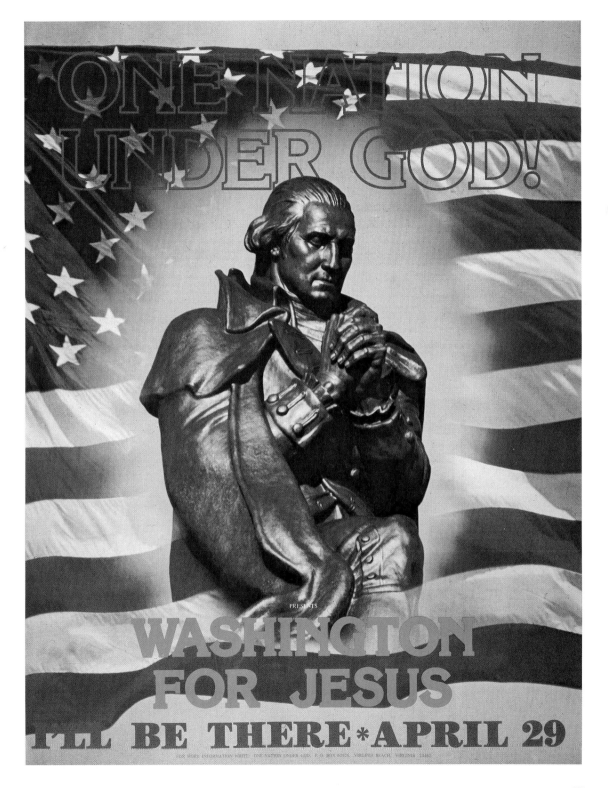

ONE NATION UNDER GOD!

PRESENTS

WASHINGTON FOR JESUS

I'LL BE THERE * APRIL 29

FOR MORE INFORMATION WRITE: ONE NATION UNDER GOD, P. O. BOX 82524, VIRGINIA BEACH, VIRGINIA 23462

EMULATED

Washington was often looked upon as a model of virtue worthy of sincere emulation. His life story was used as a pattern to inspire and instruct, and his personal character as a standard to be achieved. Washington became a model for nurturing prudence, modesty, courtesy, charity, obedience, religiosity, courage, industry, honesty, chastity, and benevolence. On occasion the image of Washington was used to inspire adults into the ways of right.

Figure 56
Ribbon of The Washington Temperance Society with a standing figure of George Washington and the legend *We bear a patriot's honored name/Our country's welfare is our aim.* The Society was founded in Baltimore in 1840.
From the Ralph E. Becker Collection,
National Museum of American History.

The exhibition also includes:

Ribbon of the Washington Temperance Benevolent Society bearing the legend *Temperance: The Handmaid and Guardian Angel of Virtue, Liberty and Independence.*
From the Ralph E. Becker Collection,
National Museum of American History.

Medal of the Washington Temperance Society with a bust of George Washington and a Temperance Declaration: *We agree to abstain from all intoxicating liquors.*
National Museum of American History.

Washington the Mediator, a print from *Harper's Weekly*, March 23, 1861. Washington is shown separating two brawling soldiers, who implicitly symbolize the North and the South.
From the Ralph E. Becker Collection,
National Museum of American History.

George Washington as a Housekeeper with Glimpses of His Domestic Arrangements, Dining, Company, etc., published by Joseph F. Sabin, New York, 1924.
From the Ralph E. Becker Collection,
National Museum of American History.

Figure 57
Dragging the Poacher Ashore, a book illustration, 19th century.
National Museum of American History.

WASHINGTON DRAGGING THE POACHER ASHORE.

THE LOVE OF TRUTH
MARK THE BOY

At six years old, George, full of boyish tricks,
Would often please himself by chopping sticks;
A friend who witnessed oft his favrite sport,
Once bought a hatchet of the smaller sort,
And made a present to the darling boy:
The welcome treasure fired his heart with joy;
With eager speed he hasted to the court,
Where faggot piles afforded harmless sport;
But wishing soon new fields of enterprize,
The high-wall'd garden next the adventurer tries;
There thoughtless running down the gravel walks,
The heads of flowers he severd from their stalks.
This error would not much have signified,
Had not the hatchet's keenest edge been tried
Upon a favourite tree—oh! fatal touch!
It bore an English cherry, valued much.

Dearly 'twas purchased, newly planted there,
To thrive for many a distant, livelong year.
George left,—perhaps unconscious of the wound,
Or else for string to tie the pieces round.
Soon after this, his Father passing by,
The shiver'd trunk directly caught his eye.
Quick rose vexation and regret to see
The hopeless ruin of his favrite tree;
Back to the house with hasty steps he ran,
The gard'ner question'd ask'd each maid and man,
But could no tidings gain; all, all, said 'No;
And sad suspence was left awhile to grow.
Just then, the little fellow met his sire:
'O!' he exclaim'd 'It is my great desire
To find the person who hath killed the tree
That yonder stands; come down with me and see.

The weapon of the deed by George was borne:
The father's heart was now with anguish torn;
He felt affection, for he loved his child,—
Dreaded to chide,—of disposition mild.
The real culprit, now so very near,
One moment thought, but shew'd no signs of fear;
His little heart with principle beat high;
'Papa, I *cannot, will not* tell a lie!
My sharp bright hatchet gave the naughty stroke.'
The parent then with love and rapture spoke,
'Run to my open arms, my dearest boy;
Your *love of truth* bespeaks a father's joy:
My sudden anger and my grief are fled,
Although my lovely cherry-tree is dead.

* Afterwards the celebrated WASHINGTON.

For the most part, Washington's image was used by adults to inspire children to virtue during their formative years. Wrote Horatio Hastings Weld in 1845, "The first word of infancy should be mother, the second father, the third WASHINGTON."

Figure 58
The Love of Truth Mark the Boy, a roller-printed cotton handkerchief with a poem recounting Parson Weems' cherry tree legend.
National Museum of American History.

The exhibition also includes:

Hatchet-shaped pin with the inscription *I cannot tell a lie.*
National Museum of American History.

Medal depicting a young George Washington with hatchet in hand beside a felled cherry tree, with the inscription *Magna Est Veritas Et Praevalebit* (Truth is great and it will prevail).
National Museum of American History.

Peddie Memorial Christmas Market ribbon, *I cannot tell a lie, I did it with my little hatchet.*
From the Ralph E. Becker Collection,
National Museum of American History.

Life of Washington, Written for Children by E. Cecil, published by P. O'Shea, New York, 1867. This copy was awarded as a *First Premium* by the School of the Immaculate Conception in Baltimore, Maryland, to Mary Lustnaeur in July 1867.
National Museum of American History.

Sunday School medal with a portrait of George Washington surrounded by the inscription, *Patriotism/Industry/Progress*, c.1876.
From the Ralph E. Becker Collection,
National Museum of American History.

Rules of Conduct by George Washington, pamphlet Number 24 in the Riverside Literature Series published by Riverside Press of Cambridge, Massachusetts, in February 1887.
National Museum of American History.

Child's tin plate with a bust of Washington encircled by the alphabet.
National Museum of American History.

Tea set made as a gift for Phoebe Apperson Hearst, the first contributor to the George Washington Memorial Association. The Association, which was organized in 1899 to raise funds for the *National University* mentioned in George Washington's Will, presented the money collected to Columbian College, Washington, D.C., with the understanding that its name would be changed to The George Washington University.
National Museum of American History.

Figure 59
Soldier-shaped pin with the inscription *Never told a lie.*
National Museum of American History.

Figure 60
Uncle Sam, a reproduction of a poster by Albert T. Reid which was used in conjunction with special juvenile activities held around the country during the 1932 celebration of the bicentennial of Washington's birth.
National Museum of American History.

The exhibition also includes:

Schoolroom Portrait, a reproduction of Gilbert Stuart's Athenaeum portrait of George Washington, was distributed to every classroom in America in 1932.
National Museum of American History.

The Pageant of A Nation, a series of lesson cards produced by the Master Library Company of Chicago, c.1930 (1960 edition). Each card features a *full color reproduction of the historical paintings of J.L.G. Ferris*, a suggested application, and questions for *younger and older pupils*. Ten cards in the series feature George Washington.
National Museum of American History.

Our Heritage, by Norman Rockwell, 1950. Oil on canvas, $41\frac{1}{2}'' \times 31\frac{1}{2}''$.
Painted for a Boy Scout calendar.
Lent by the National Office, Boy Scouts of America.

Pocketknife and wrapper, a modern souvenir produced by the George Washington Masonic National Memorial after the original which, tradition holds, Mary Ball Washington gave to her son George as a reminder that he should always *obey his superiors*.
National Museum of American History.

Woven arm patch with portrait of George Washington: *The Father of Our Country*.
National Museum of American History.

George Washington's Cherry Tree and a silhouette of George Washington, projects made by elementary school children to mark George Washington's birthday, 1979.
National Museum of American History.

Figure 61
Beetle Bailey comic strip by Mort Walker, the artist's original for a strip published August 28, 1980.
National Museum of American History; gift of Mort Walker.

MONUMENTALIZED

George Washington, feet on the ground, was a man. George Washington on the pedestal is sculpture, an image looming cold, unfeeling, untouchable. He has been made mute, bleached, colorless, and upon him are projected images changing with our needs. We have made him a monument.

In the process of monumentalizing George Washington we have stripped him of his humanity. We have made him so abstract that we now often view him with unease. We poke fun at the monument by making jokes and delighting in stories of his foibles, but the blasphemy itself reveals the underlying belief. There is something about George Washington that persistently intrigues us— perhaps because we know that at the core of the monument we have created there was George Washington, a human being.

Figure 62
Marble statue of George Washington by Horatio Greenough, 1841.
National Museum of American Art.

PART II

G. Washington "TAKING CARE TO PERFORM THE PARTS ASSIGNED"

"TAKING CARE TO PERFORM THE PARTS ASSIGNED"

George Washington viewed the world as a theatre and all the men and women in it as players. From his youth, he saw himself as a figure upon that stage, and he sought to play his roles in the "scenes" of life with "a perfect, unvarying constancy of character to the very last act." No matter what the place or the role, Washington hoped always to be able "to close the drama with applause," and ultimately "to retire from the theatre with the . . . approbation of angels and men."

Figure 63
Plaster bust of Washington made by Clark Mills in 1853 from the original life cast made by Jean Antoine Houdon at Mount Vernon. On October 2, 1785 George Washington recorded in his diary the arrival of *Mr. Houdon, sent from Paris by Doctr. Franklin and Mr. Jefferson to take my Bust, in behalf of the State of Virginia.* Because it was cast by the famous French sculptor from a life mask, the bust accurately captures a sense of George Washington, the man. *National Museum of American History.*

THE BEGINNING

*In the year 1657 or thereabouts, and during the
Usurpation of Oliver Cromwell—*

*John and Lawrence Washington, Brothers,
Emigrated from the North of England, and settled at
Bridges Creek, on Potomac River, in the County of
Westmoreland.*

*John Washington . . . married Ann Pope, and left
issue two Sons, Lawrence and John, and one daughter
Ann.*

*Lawrence Washington, his eldest son, married
Mildred Warner . . . of Gloucester County, by whom
he had two Sons, John and Augustine and one
daughter named Mildred.*

*Augustine, son of Lawrence and Mildred Warner,
married Jane Butler, Jane, wife of Augustine, died . . .*

*Augustine then married Mary Ball, March 6, 1730:
by whom he had issue George . . . .*

*—George Washington to Sir Isaac Heard
May 2, 1792*

The exhibition also includes:

Froe, broad hoe, narrow hoe, felling ax, and sickle
blade found at the site of John Washington's Popes
Creek farm in Westmoreland County, Virginia.
*Lent by the George Washington Birthplace National
Monument, National Park Service.*

Eighteenth century plow, Northumberland County,
Virginia.
National Museum of American History.

THE PLACE AND TIME

The first Washington to come to America was
John, a mate on the London-based ketch "Sea
Horse," who arrived in Virginia in 1657 as an
impoverished adventurer without any sort of
property. He soon married the dowered
daughter of a well-to-do landholder, however,
and began to acquire land, the source of
wealth and standing. Through headright
claims, purchase, and favored dealings with
the colony's powerful elite this shrewd but
somewhat unscrupulous entrepreneur built
up both his holdings and his social standing.

By the time John's grandson Augustine
Washington came of age in 1715, the family's
position as respected members of the
Virginia gentry was secure. Three generations
of Washingtons had increased the family's
holdings in personal property, slaves, and
land well beyond those of the average
colonial. All the Washingtons had counted
among their friends and neighbors some of the
most powerful members of the gentry. All had
served variously as officers in the militia; as
tax collectors, sheriffs, House of Burgesses
representatives, court justices; and as
vestrymen in the established church.

Augustine continued the family pattern,
serving as church warden and sheriff and
adding some 9000 acres of land and well over
£1500 in personal property to his holdings at a
time when an average farmer in the colony
owned 20 acres of land and £16 worth of
goods. On the eve of George Washington's
birth, his father Augustine was among the
most established and affluent of the gentry
in his Popes Creek neighborhood.

Figure 64
View of Popes Creek from the site of the
Washington farm, Westmoreland County, Virginia.
*Courtesy of the Smithsonian Institution Photographic
Services Division.*

BIRTH OF A BABY

George Washington was born to Augustine Washington and his second wife, Mary Ball Washington, on February 22 in 1732. As this event occurred two decades before the reform of the calendar by which all dates were moved ahead eleven days, his birth date is recorded in the family Bible as February 11. Formal affiliation with the Anglican Church was the first step in establishing the child as a member of the Virginia gentry. George was baptized soon after his birth, and he remained a member of the Church until his death.

Figure 65
Infant's robe of white brocaded silk lined with old-rose china silk, used on the occasion of George Washington's christening.
From the Lewis Collection,
National Museum of American History.

The exhibition also includes:

Mary Ball Washington's Bible. On a sheet of paper affixed to one of the pages she recorded the birth of George Washington: *George Washington Son to Augustine & Mary his wife was Born ye 11th Day of February 1731/2 about 10 in the Morning and was Baptised the 15th of April following Mr. Beverley Whiting & Capt. Christopher Brooks Godfathers and Mrs Mildred Gregory Godmother.*
Lent by the Mount Vernon Ladies' Association.

THE FORMATIVE MILIEU

The Virginia Colony was a small world in which members of the upper class modeled themselves after the gentry in England and struggled somewhat clumsily to achieve their aspirations in a provincial wilderness. George Washington grew up surrounded by people and institutions which channeled newcomers, either youths or arrivals, into modes of behavior appropriate to the gentry in Virginia.

Members of this class shared a particular personal and public style and rigidly defined conceptions of private and civic duty. Entry was quite open to persons of wealth who adopted this behavior—and a hasty exit was equally possible for those who lost their wealth or failed to behave "properly." Male members of the gentry had to be genteel in bearing, "polish'd" in conversation, and neat in appearance. They had to surround themselves with the proper trappings and pursue the established recreations. They were expected to be generous in their hospitality to their peers and liberal in their treatment of those of a lesser social level. Duty required them to be self-assertive, to protect their personal and family honor, and to assume positions of military, political, and economic leadership both within their neighborhoods and, when appropriate, in the colony as a whole.

As a boy immersed in this world, George Washington unconsciously absorbed many of the notions and values of the genteel order through observation of his family, their friends, and the larger colonial community. He seems to have consciously recognized the importance of fulfilling his class-designated role relatively early in his life. While he was still in his teens he began to actively mold himself into the kind of person he would have to be in order to achieve not only the respect of his peers, but also a sense of self-esteem.

TRUE HAPPINESS

These are the things which once Possess'd
Will make a life thats truly bless'd
A Good Estate on healthy Soil
Not got by Vice, nor yet by Toil:
Round a warm Fire, a Pleasant Joke,
With Chimney ever free from Smoke:
A Strength entire, A Sparkling Bowl,
A quiet Wife a quiet Soul,
A Mind as well as body, whole
Prudent Simplicity, constant Friends,
A diet which no art Commends;
A Merry Night without much Drinking
A Happy Thought without much Thinking;
Each Night by Quiet Sleep made Short
A Will to be but what thou art:
Possess'd of these, all else defy
And neither wish nor fear to Die.
—George Washington in his Copy Book, 1745

AUGUSTINE: "MY FATHER"

Augustine Washington was three years old when his father died. His mother soon married an English businessman and the family moved to England, where Augustine attended Appleby School, a preparatory academy. When his mother died he was brought back to Virginia to live with an uncle.

Augustine had been left a respectable estate and soon after he came of age he married Jane Butler, by whom he had four children—Lawrence and Augustine, who survived, and Jane and Butler, who died as children. After his first wife died suddenly in 1730, Augustine married Mary Ball.

Augustine Washington shared with his grandfather and with other Virginia gentlemen a passion for land acquisition and business ventures extending far beyond the limits of his small farm at Popes Creek. Like other Virginia gentlemen of that era, Augustine also developed an interest in exploiting the mineral wealth of the Virginia Colony. When iron ore was found on land he owned at remote Accokeek Creek in 1724, he saw an opportunity to further diversify his holdings and thereby tap a new source of income. He entered into an agreement with the Principio Iron Company, a group of English investors already operating in Maryland, to mine and process the ore.

When George was three years old, Augustine moved his family further north along the Potomac River to land on Little Hunting Creek, nearer the mine. When Augustine became personally involved in the operation of the mine three years later, he moved his family still closer, to Ferry Farm, near Fredericksburg, Virginia, where George spent the rest of his youth.

The death of his father in 1743 had an ever-widening impact on the life of eleven-year old George. The most immediate effect was that, because of financial and family insecurities resulting from Augustine's death, George would not be able to attend school in England as had his two older half-brothers. Neither would George have the benefit of a father's advice and social connections as he sought to establish himself as a fledgling member of the gentry. Then, too, the distribution of Augustine's estate gave the choicest property to George's half-brothers. His share—Ferry Farm, a half interest in another 4000-acre tract of poor land, and ten slaves—was meager by comparison.

George's genetic inheritance from his father—above average height and physical strength—and his equestrian aptitude were attributes that would serve him well in a society that valued athletic skills and physical prowess. It was clear that with his father dead, however, George would have to achieve gentlemanly status and its requisite financial means as best he could on his own. This prospect weighed heavily on the boy, who by his teens had already recognized how importantly that genteel role figured in both the respect of his peers and his own self-esteem. Washington's desire to establish himself as a member of the Virginia gentry would determine in large measure his thought and action in the years that followed. To others, his diligence in these efforts would seem somewhat over-anxious and on occasion—especially during his youth—even crude.

The exhibition also includes:

Map showing the division of the land on Little Hunting Creek between John Spencer and John Washington, 1690. This property was eventually acquired by Augustine Washington in 1735.
Lent by the Mount Vernon Ladies' Association.

Pieces of iron ore found at the site of the Accokeek iron works.
National Museum of American History.

Letter to John England, Ironmaster in the colonies, from partners of the Principio Company in England, September 15, 1725. By this writing England was empowered *to build iron works on Captain Washington's land* and to *try ye Captains mine [ore] in ye furnaces as soon as ye can.*
Lent by the Maryland Historical Society, Manuscripts Division; gift of James B. England.

Deed tripartite between Augustine Washington and members of the Principio Company, dated March 2, 1729. The deed notes that *an iron furnace, dam, and other works and buildings for the roasting of iron* had been erected on Washington's Accokeek property, for which he was to receive one-sixth of the resulting profits.
Lent by the Maryland Historical Society, Manuscripts Division; gift of James B. England.

A Complete View of British Customs, by Henry Crouch, 1731. Augustine Washington purchased this book on May 4, 1737, when he was in England conferring with members of the Principio Iron Company.
Lent by the Boston Athenaeum.

Figure 66
Iron fireback from the house at Ferry Farm bearing the initials of Augustine and Mary Washington, 1734. The date suggests that the fireback was made with iron from the Accokeek furnace.
From the Virginia Room,
Daughters of the American Revolution Museum.

MARY: "HON'D MADAM"

Mary Ball Washington, George's mother, had been orphaned at an early age. She was three years old when her father died and fourteen when her mother died, leaving her to the care of relatives who were comparative strangers. Mary had inherited land, livestock, and slaves from her father, and from her mother she received control of an entire estate. This financial security perhaps reinforced her sense of self-reliance, but her early emotional deprivation left her self-oriented and insecure. She was an independent woman who kept herself in control and who sought control of those around her.

Mary was twenty-four when she married Augustine Washington in 1731. She gave birth to George a year later, then to Betty in 1733, Samuel in 1734, John Augustine in 1736, Charles in 1737, and Mildred in 1739.

It seems likely that she and George were never very affectionate. When he was young, she was much occupied with the younger children. As the sole parental power after Augustine's death, she was strong-willed and demanding. George, himself resolute in the midst of adolescence, was often at odds with her. He did not understand her interference with his first efforts to strike out on his own, and he struggled with her continuing control over his share of the inheritance from his father (he would wait thirty years before receiving his allotment). His early frustration perhaps contributed to the readiness and zest with which he pursued his ambitions.

Although his mother was often a trial to George, he was careful during her lifetime to honor the filial obligations which were mandatory to a member of the gentry. When she died, he refused to part with her small legacies to him, saying he considered them "mementos of parental affection in the last solemn act of life" and that he "set a value on them much beyond their intrinsic worth."

The exhibition also includes:

Letter from Joseph Ball to Mary Ball Washington, May 19, 1747. When, at the age of fifteen, George had wanted to join the Royal Navy, his mother refused to allow him to leave Ferry Farm. In this letter, his uncle warns that the navy would *use him like a Negro, or rather like a dog.*
Lent by the Library of Congress.

Model of British ship of the line of the type on which George Washington would have sailed.
National Museum of American History.

Sandalwood fan owned by Mary Ball Washington.
Lent by the Mary Washington House.

Mourning brooch owned by Mary Ball Washington.
National Museum of American History.

Book of Meditations with the signature of Mary Ball.
Lent by the Mary Washington House.

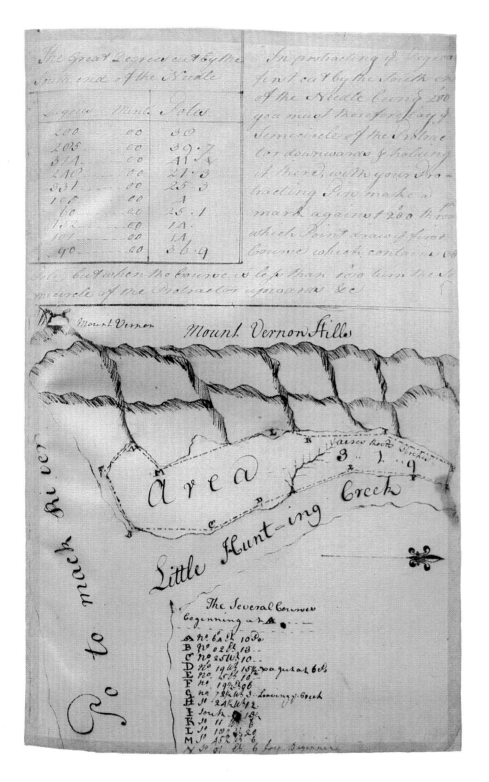

HIS EDUCATION: "VERY USEFUL AND NECESSARY"

In the Virginia colony the children of the gentry who were not sent to schools in England were taught at home by private tutors. Although little is known about George Washington's formal education, he was probably instructed by tutors available in the Fredericksburg area. Under their guidance, he studied penmanship, spelling, the "very useful and Necessary Branch[es] of the Mathematick," surveying, geography, and astronomy.

Figure 67
Surveying exercise in George Washington's Second School Copy Book, 1747/8.
Lent by the Library of Congress.

George's formal education was not extensive, and a family friend observed that it "might have been bettered." George was deliberate of mind, however; "method and exactness" came naturally to him, and in his own persistent and methodical way he constantly observed and learned from the world around him. He learned a great deal from the members of his own family—especially his half-brothers, who had been educated in England—as well as from friends of the family and his own experiences. This informal education augmented his tutored studies; more important, it equipped him with the social graces and a concrete sense of the role and obligations of a colonial gentleman. "He is, in my judgment," wrote a family friend, "a man who will go to school all his life and profit thereby."

Washington retained respect for—and perhaps an envy of—formal education all of his life. In his Will and Testament he left money to several schools, including the Academy in the town of Alexandria for the support of a free school to educate orphan children and the "children of such other poor and indigent persons as are unable to accomplish it with their own means." He also left a bequest to be used toward the endowment of a university in the central part of the United States "to which youths of fortune and talent from all parts thereof might be sent for completion of their education."

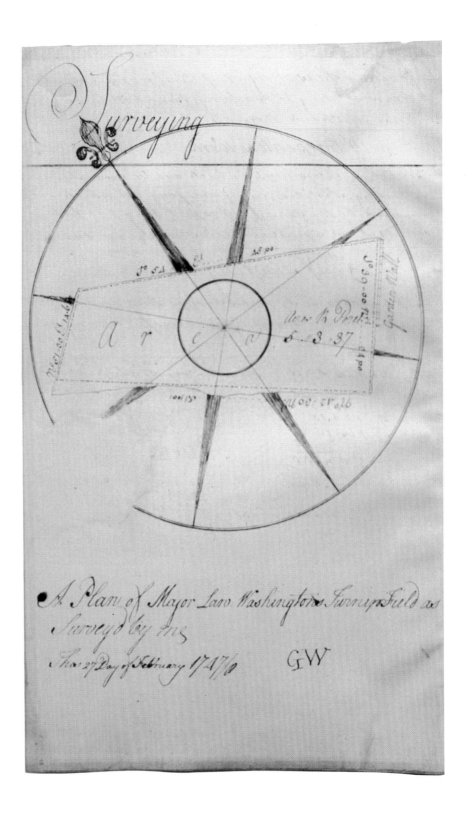

Figure 68
A Plan of Major Law. Washington's Turnip Field as Survey'd by me, in George Washington's Second School Copy Book, 1747/8.
Lent by the Library of Congress.

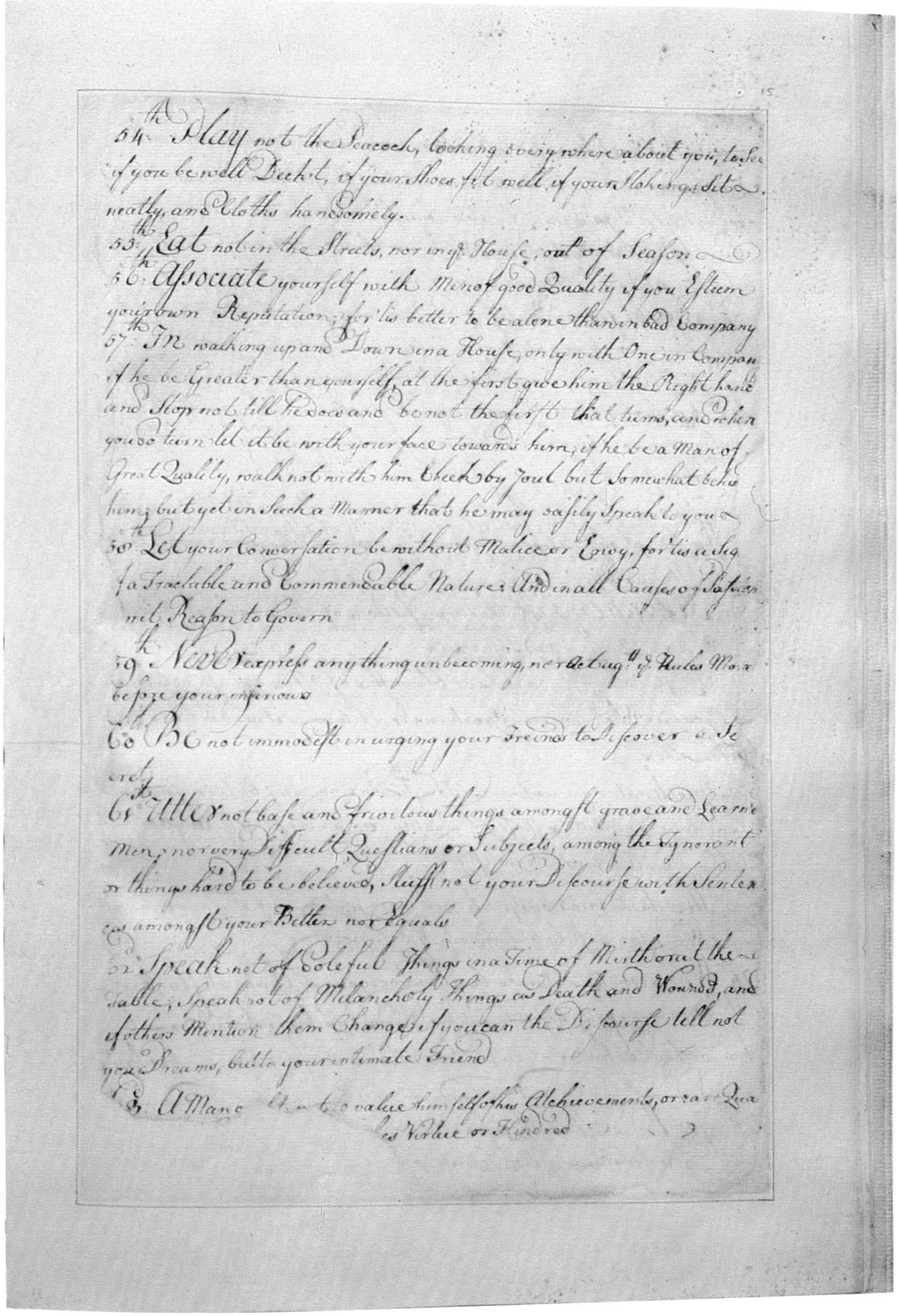

54th Play not the Peacock, looking every where about you, to see if you be well Deck't, if your Shoes fit well if your Stokings sit neatly, and Cloths handsomely.

55th Eat not in the Streets, nor in yͤ House, out of Season

56 Associate yourself with Men of good Quality if you Esteem your own Reputation; for 'tis better to be alone than in bad Company

57th In walking up and Down in a House, only with One in Company if he be Greater than yourself, at the first give him the Right hand and Stop not till he does and be not the first that turns, and when you do turn let it be with your face towards him, if he be a Man of Great Quality, walk not with him Cheek by Joul but Somewhat behind him; but yet in Such a Manner that he may easily Speak to you

58th Let your Conversation be without Malice or Envy, for 'tis a Sign of a Tractable and Commendable Nature: And in all Causes of Passion admit Reason to Govern

59th Never express any thing unbecoming, nor Act agtͭ yͤ Rules Moral before your inferiours

60 Be not immodest in urging your Freinds to Discover a Secret

61 Utter not base and frivolous things amongst grave and Learn'd Men, nor very Difficult Questions or Subjects, among the Ignorant or things hard to be believed, Stuff not your Discourse with Sentences amongst your Betters nor Equals

62 Speak not of doleful Things in a Time of Mirth or at the Table; Speak not of Melancholy Things as Death and Wounds, and if others Mention them Change if you can the Discourse tell not your Dreams, but to your intimate Friend

63 A Man [ought] not to value himself of his Achievements, or rare Qualities of wit; much less of his riches Virtue or Kindred

Figure 69
Rules of Civility and Decent Behaviour in Company and Conversation. Washington copied these customs of the *Better Bred* into his school copy book.
Lent by the Library of Congress.

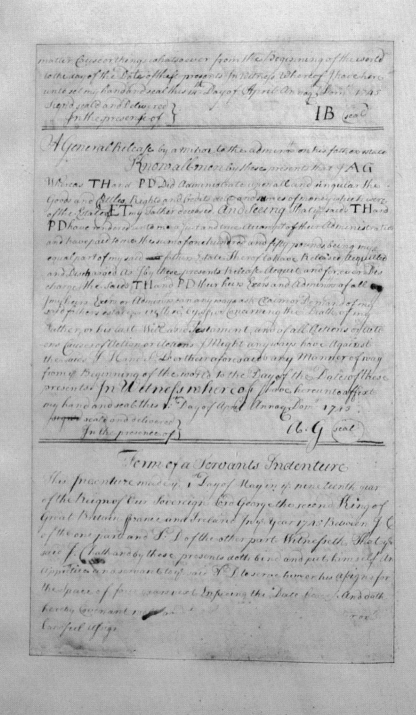

Figure 70
Business forms and legal instruments copied by
George Washington into his school copybook.
Lent by the Library of Congress.

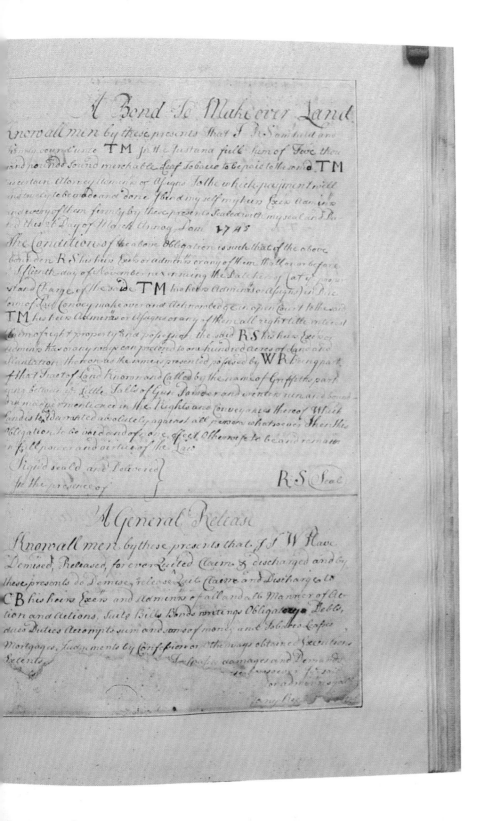

The exhibition also includes:

Drafting tools used by George Washington.
Lent by the Mount Vernon Ladies' Association.

LAWRENCE: "DEAR BROTHER"

Figure 71
Portrait of Lawrence Washington, by an unknown
artist, possibly English, 1738.
Oil on canvas, $30\frac{1}{2}'' \times 27''$.
Lent by the Mount Vernon Ladies' Association.

Lawrence Washington, the first-born son
of Augustine and his first wife, was
already a young man away at school in
England when George was born. When
he returned to Virginia at the age of
twenty, Lawrence's dashing glamour,
gentlemanly grace, urbanity, and charm
left the impressionable six-year-old
George spellbound.

At the age of twenty-two, Lawrence
became an officer in a Virginia regiment
that sailed to join Admiral Edward
Vernon of the Royal British Navy in an
assault on the Spanish at the Caribbean
port of Cartagena. George was
captivated by his half-brother's red
uniform, and became enamored of the
glory and adventure of a military
career.

By the time Augustine died in 1743,
Lawrence was already a well-established
member of the gentry. He became his
younger brother's best friend and
primary role model, including George
in many of his activities. George was
soon practicing the gentlemanly style.
By the time he was sixteen he was
carefully shaving every day and taking
care to dress properly; on one trip his
luggage included nine clean shirts.

Upon Augustine's death, Lawrence
had inherited the family estate at
Little Hunting Creek, which he
renamed Mount Vernon in honor of
the Admiral. Here, where Lawrence
lived with his wife Ann, George could
escape from the trials of residing with
an overbearing mother and five younger
siblings. Here, too, he could savor the
life of the gentry. George attended
frequent dances, shooting matches,
barbecues and races, and clubbed with
other gentlemen, partaking of peach
brandy and passing the time in games
of loo and whist.

Not illustrated in catalog:

License of Richard Yates, headmaster when George Washington's brothers Lawrence and Augustine attended Appleby School.
Lent by courtesy of the Governors, the Grammar School, Appleby, Cumbria, England.

Letter to Lawrence Washington from Richard Yates, November 13, 1743, congratulating him on his marriage to Ann Fairfax.
Lent by the Morristown National Historical Park, National Park Service.

Figure 72
Drawing of the headmaster's house at Appleby School showing the doorway of the original building, where Lawrence Washington attended school, by E. Threlkeld, c.1880.
Watercolor on paper, $10\frac{1}{2}'' \times 12\frac{3}{4}''$.
Lent by courtesy of the Governors, the Grammar School, Appleby, Cumbria, England.

When Lawrence's health began to deteriorate, he selected George to accompany him to Barbados. At his death, in 1752, George was named as residual heir to Mount Vernon if both Lawrence's wife and their only surviving child died. These seemed remote contingencies, but after the death of the child in 1754 George rented Mount Vernon; in 1761, the death of Lawrence's widow made him the estate's owner.

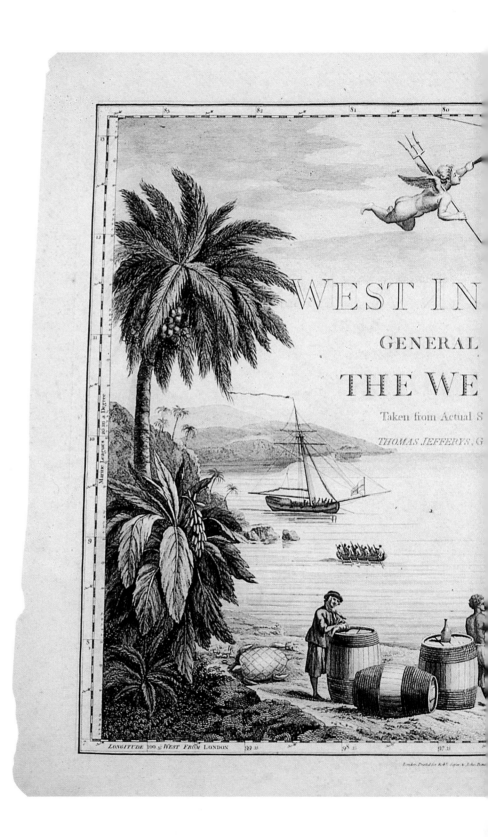

Figure 73

The West Indian Atlas, by Thomas Jefferys, Geographer to the King, 1775. When George Washington accompanied his brother Lawrence to Barbados he was *perfectly enraptured with the beautiful prospects, which every side presented to our view—the field of cane, corn, fruit trees, etc. in a delightful green.*
Lent by the Library of Congress.

The exhibition also includes:

Lease to land at Little Hunting Creek (Mount Vernon) from Ann, widow of Lawrence, to George Washington, December 15, 1754.
Lent by John F. Fleming.

THE FAMILY AT BELVOIR: "MY INTIMATE FRIENDS"

I should be glad to hear you live in Harmony and good fellowship with the family at Belvoir as it is in their power to be very serviceable . . . upon many occasions to us as young beginners. I would advise your visiting often as one step towards it . . . for to that Family I am under many obligations.
    —George Washington to his brother Jack
    May 28, 1755

Lawrence's estate at Mount Vernon was an isolated outpost of civilization on the northern fringe of settlement along the Potomac River. It was a fortunate happenstance that the adjoining estate at Belvoir belonged to William Fairfax, kinsman and agent of Thomas, Lord Fairfax. Lord Fairfax was the proprietor of a royal land grant that encompassed all of the Northern Neck westward into the Alleghany Mountains— some five million acres. In his vast personal colony within the Virginia colony, the wealthy Fairfax reigned supreme, and his family constituted the highest level of society.

Lawrence Washington came to know the Fairfaxes well as neighbors, and eventually married Ann Fairfax, William's daughter, thus joining the whirl of occupation and recreation that was a way of life for the colony's ruling families. When young George visited his brother, he was accepted as a member of the Fairfax family and included in their activities. The gangly teenager revelled in the elegance and leisure of aristocratic life. He was fascinated, indeed enchanted, by the Fairfaxes' witty and cosmpolitan conversation and by their extensive circle of powerful and engaging friends.

For their part, the Fairfaxes were fond of the young man who was so appreciative of their worldliness and flattered by his eager emulation of their ways. George thrived under their tutelage. Their friendship facilitated his pursuit of gentlemanly status: they provided social introductions and helped him acquire the financial means requisite to high social position.

The charm of the Fairfax world was made even more enthralling for George by the friendship of Sally, the wife of George William Fairfax, his constant and steadfast companion. With light grey-blue eyes and auburn hair, Washington was presumably quite presentable, but he was as awkward and self-conscious as any other sixteen-year old. The attention of a beautiful older woman (she was eighteen) of the genteel sort proved particularly enchanting.

Figure 74

A survey of the Northern Neck of Virginia, being the Lands belonging to the Rt. Honorable Thomas Lord Fairfax, by John Warner. Printed on vellum from an engraved copperplate (fourth state), c.1747. *Lent by the Library of Congress.*

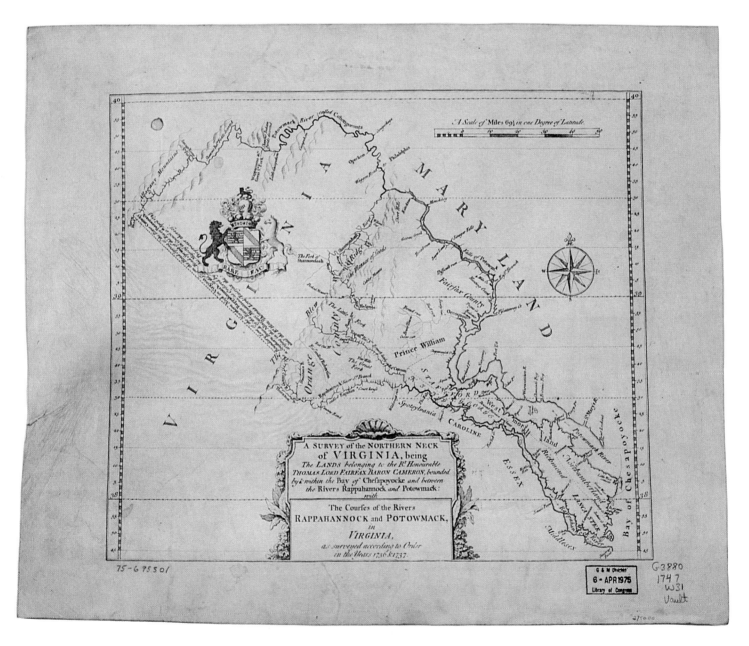

Figure 75
Green silk coat trimmed with silver lace which
belonged to Thomas, Lord Fairfax.
*Lent by the National Society of the Colonial Dames
of America.*

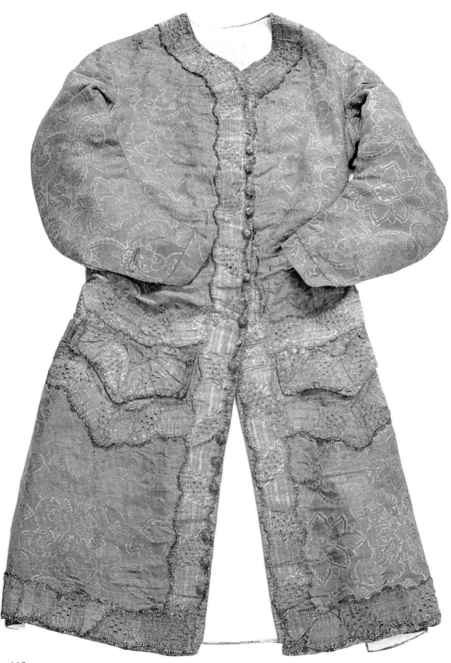

The exhibition also includes:

Grant for land issued in 1751 by Thomas, Lord Fairfax, to Francis Thorton of Caroline County, Virginia.
National Museum of American History.

Iron strongbox in which Thomas, Lord Fairfax, safeguarded his hard cash and negotiable papers.
Lent by the Shenandoah Valley National Bank.

Desk of Colonel George William Fairfax, Belvoir. Mahogany, American, 1769-73.
Lent from a private collection.

Commission from George William Fairfax to George Washington to survey *Grubbs Entry near Bull Skin,* 1750.
Lent by the Library of Congress.

Figure 76
Silver candlesticks displaying the Fairfax crest, which were among the household furnishings at Belvoir. London, 1762-63. Emrick Roemer, silversmith.
Lent from a family collection.

THE SURVEYS: "A GOOD REWARD . . .
IS MY CONSTANT GAIN EVERY DAY"

The orderly George Washington was from his youth fascinated by surveying—the laying of a measured grid upon raw topography. His earliest surviving school exercises were in the "Mensuration of Superficies." He drew his first survey, a plate of Lawrence's turnip patch, when he was sixteen. That same year he and young George William Fairfax traveled to the frontier as part of a party of surveyors hired to lay out the Fairfax lands in the Shenandoah Valley.

In 1749, when George was seventeen, he secured his first job—assisting a surveyor in plotting the town of Alexandria—through his Fairfax connections. Fairfax influence also led to his appointment as an official surveyor for Culpeper County a few months later. By the spring of 1750, less than a year after his first warranted survey, he had saved enough cash to purchase his first tract of land.

This purchase was especially significant to George Washington because in the Virginia colony ownership of land brought the wealth and social status to which he aspired. He used his position as surveyor to scout out areas of unclaimed land and to accumulate money to purchase the rich tracts by which he could ultimately support his status as a gentleman.

Surveying provided obvious economic benefits, but it afforded important social and political opportunities as well. Surveyors, whose knowledge of land was so crucial to the economic well-being of the gentry, were welcomed in the highest social circles of the colony. George took full advantage of this access. He soon won the favor of many of the colony's wealthiest and most influential families. Through his painstakingly accurate surveys and his pleasant and proper social behavior, he was beginning to achieve not only the respect of his peers, but a sense of self-esteem as well.

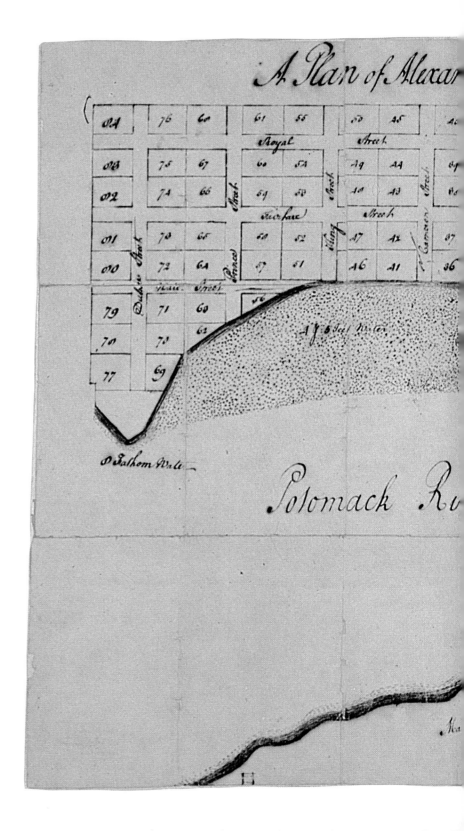

Figure 77

A Plan of Alexandria, now Belhaven made
by George Washington in 1749.
Lent by the Library of Congress.

Figure 78
Notes of Surveys, a field notebook kept by George Washington, 1749-50.
Lent by the Library of Congress.

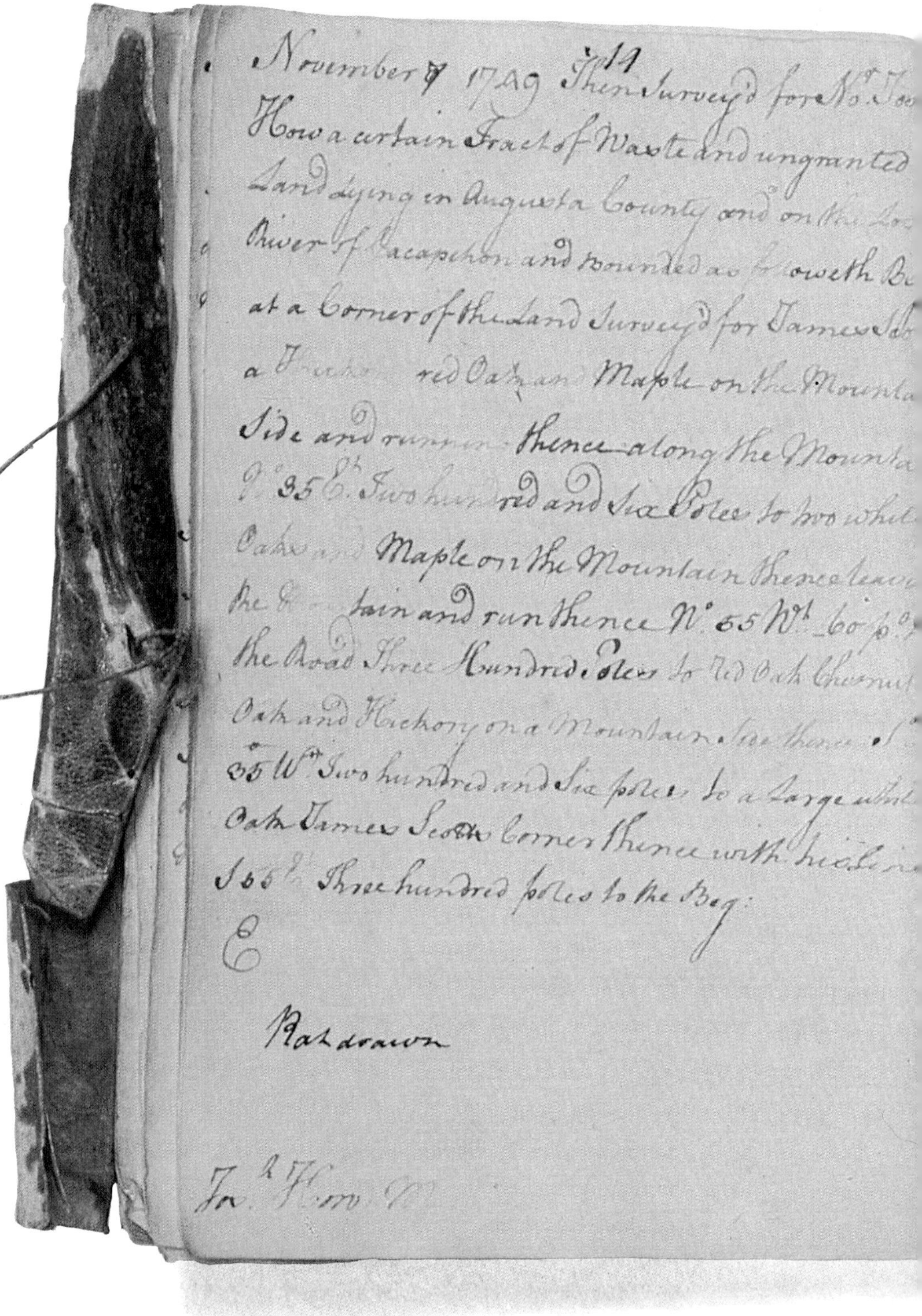
November 7 1749 Then Survey'd for No. Jo...
How a certain Tract of Waste and ungranted
Land lying in Augusta County and on the ...
River of Cacapehon and bounded as followeth Be...
at a Corner of the Land Survey'd for James Sco...
a ... red Oak and Maple on the Mounta...
Side and running thence along the Mounta...
N° 35 Et. Two hundred and Six Poles to two whit...
Oaks and Maple on the Mountain thence leav...
the Mountain and run thence N° 55 Wt. 60 p°...
the Road Three Hundred Poles to Red Oak Chesnut
Oak and Hickory on a Mountain Side thence S...
35 Wt. Two hundred and Six poles to a Large whit...
Oak James Scotts Corner thence with his line
S 55 ... Three hundred poles to the Beg:
E

Rat drawn

Jon. Howe ...

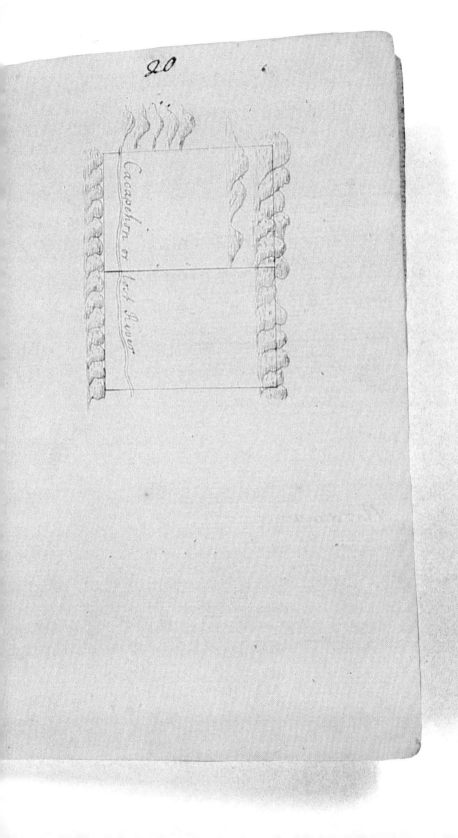

The exhibition also includes:

Stem for a calumet (peace pipe) that George Washington smoked with an Indian chief during his first *Journey Over the Mountains 1747/8.*
National Museum of American History.

Pursuant to a Warrant from the Proprietors Office, George Washington made this survey of *a certain tract of waste and ungranted land in Frederick County* [Virginia], 1750.
Lent by the Library of Congress.

Surveying compass and staff of the type used by George Washington.
Lent by the Mount Vernon Ladies' Association.

THE FIRST STEPS

You have now arrived at that age when you must quit the trifling amusements of a boy, and assume the more dignified manners of a man.

It is therefore absolutely necessary, if you mean to make any figure upon the stage, that you should take the first steps right.

—George Washington to
George Steptoe Washington
March 23, 1789

THE COMMAND: "MUCH DEARER THAN THE PAY"

The glamour of Lawrence's military service had made a strong impression on George. As a boy he had been captivated by the drama of his older brother's service at Cartagena, and as an adolescent he had noted the prestige that accompanied Lawrence's position as Adjutant General in the Virginia militia.

When Lawrence died and the adjutancy was broken into four separate jurisdictions, George applied for one of the commands. "To gain by it," he wrote, "is the least of my expectations." His well-placed friends provided the necessary political leverage, and at the age of twenty he was granted a commission as commanding officer of one of the militia districts.

In 1753, King George II—distressed by reports that the French were trespassing on English claims west of the Blue Ridge Mountains—instructed Virginia's Lieutenant Governor, Robert Dinwiddie, to send an emissary into the wilderness to order the French off British soil. Washington, learning of the planned mission through his Fairfax connections, seized the opportunity and volunteered to deliver the royal decree. The winter expedition across the mountains and almost to the Great Lakes was perilous, but despite snow, icy rivers, unfriendly Indians, and accidents, Washington accomplished his mission.

Washington's account of the trip was immediately released as a pamphlet in both Virginia and England, and within a few months his name had become identified with courageous wilderness service. It was only natural, then, that the following spring Washington was appointed Lieutenant Colonel, second-in-command of an army charged with enforcing the royal order. And so, the twenty-two year old officer with no experience in logistics, tactics, or any of the wiles of war went with a force of inexperienced men to do battle against the French. After the death of the Commander in June, Washington was left in charge of the regiment.

The campaign, a disaster from start to finish, culminated in a defeat by the French at Great Meadows, and Washington returned to stinging criticism. "Washington & many Such may have courage & resolution," wrote a British official, "but they have no Knowledge or Experience in our Profession; consequently there can be no dependence on them!" The raw American army had embarrassed the Crown, but fellow Virginians attached no blame to Washington or his army. The General Assembly of the House of Burgesses voted thanks "for their late gallent and brave behaviour in defence of their country." The royal government, however, decided to send British Army regulars from England to deal with the French. Washington resigned.

When Major General Edward Braddock and two British regiments arrived in the winter of 1755, George Washington was at Mount Vernon. He wrote a letter of welcome to Braddock and within a month the General, recognizing the value of Washington's knowledge of the terrain and wilderness experience, invited him to join his official family. The battle against the French and the Indians at the Monongahela was a calamity for the British, but Washington emerged from the fray acclaimed. He was named Colonel of the newly organized Virginia Regiment.

The Journal of Major George Washington, pamphlet
containing the report of Washington's mission
*to the Commandant of the French Forces on the
Ohio*, 1754.
*Lent by the John Carter Brown Library,
Brown University.*

The exhibition also includes:

George Washington's personal ledger recorded the
receipt of his salary as Adjutant from the Colony of
Virginia. The *1752, Oct 25* date Washington gave
the entry is a year too early, presumably due to a
slip of the pen. Washington was not commissioned
until December, 1752.
Lent by the Library of Congress.

Letter from George Washington to the Speaker of
the House of Burgesses, October 23, 1754,
acknowledging the Burgesses' thanks for *our
Behavior in the late unsuccessful Engagement with
the French at the Great Meadows.*
Lent by the Library of Congress.

General Edward Braddock's red silk military sash.
As Braddock lay mortally wounded after a clash
with the French near the Monongahela River, he
gave George Washington, his only unwounded
aide, his sash as a token of esteem.
Lent by the Mount Vernon Ladies' Association.

THE

JOURNAL

O F

Major *George Washington,*

SENT BY THE

Hon. *ROBERT DINWIDDIE,* Esq;
His Majesty's Lieutenant-Governor, and
Commander in Chief of *VIRGINIA,*

TO THE

COMMANDANT

OF THE

FRENCH FORCES

ON

OHIO.

TO WHICH ARE ADDED, THE

GOVERNOR's LETTER,

AND A TRANSLATION OF THE

FRENCH OFFICER's ANSWER.

WILLIAMSBURG:

Printed by WILLIAM HUNTER. 1754.

Figure 80
Gilded brass gorget which Washington wore as a
sign of rank during his service as an officer in the
Virginia Regiment. He is wearing the gorget in
Charles Willson Peale's 1772 portrait.
Lent by the Massachusetts Historical Society.

Portrait of George Washington in the uniform he
wore as a Virginia Colonel, by John Gadsby
Chapman, 1834, after the original by Charles
Willson Peale, 1772.
Oil on canvas, $50'' \times 39\frac{1}{2}''$.
*Lent by the West Point Museum,
U.S. Military Academy.*

Figure 81
*On exhibit by special courtesy of Washington and Lee
University, Lexington, Virginia, during June and
July 1982:*
The original Virginia Colonel portrait, by Charles
Willson Peale, 1772.
Oil on canvas, $51'' \times 42''$.

THE MATTER OF RANK: "OBLIGED TO SERVE UPON SUCH DIFFERENT TERMS"

Washington had long been intrigued by the glamour of professional soldiering and by the prospect of the social and financial advancement which came so easily to successful British officers of the time. At the outset of his military career, he had been anxious to secure a place in the regular British army in service to "our gracious King." After his service with Braddock, Washington's desire for a royal commission that would make him a British officer became stronger yet. As a member of the General's official family, Washington had become close to Braddock's aide, Captain Robert Orme. The captain, a man of about Washington's own age, had embodied everything for which the young Virginian hungered—the glamour, worldliness, prestige and self-esteem of a British officer, and the possibility of such triumphant success as that which early in the century made John Churchill, a simple English farmer turned military hero, the nationally acclaimed Duke of Marlborough.

Figure 82
Portrait of Captain Robert Orme of the British Army, by Sir Joshua Reynolds, 1756.
Oil on canvas, 95″ × 58″.
Orme, an aide to General Braddock, became a close friend of George Washington.
Lent by the National Gallery, London.

From the time of his first service with the Virginia colonial troops, however, Washington had encountered the distinction made by the British military establishment between soldiers in service to the British army and those serving in the Virginia line. Although they were fulltime professionals with a frontier to protect, the colonial soldiers were viewed with disdain. They were expected to serve with the British regulars and to assume the same risks, but they were not accorded the same salary or respect.

Washington found it unjust and intolerable that the "lives of his Majesty's subjects in Virginia should be of less value." Moreover, it affronted his personal honor that even as a commanding officer of the gentlemanly class he was not given the deference attendant to command in the British army. Any low-level British officer of lesser social standing with a commission from the Crown could command Washington's obedience.

Washington, always concerned with position and reputation, was continually tempted to "obey the call of Honour" and resign from military service; he did in fact threaten to resign seven times. Yet, although his was a position from which he expected "to reap neither honor or benefit," he retained his command. Instead of resigning, he did everything he could to curry "preferment in a military way" both for his troops and for himself. He traveled to Boston and then to Philadelphia for audiences with British military officials, and he wrote numerous letters promoting the Virginia Regiment and seeking its improved status.

Washington was continually rebuffed in his efforts to obtain either respect for his troops or a royal commission for himself. After repeated insults, Washington became disillusioned with the British military and aware of the unbridgeable separateness of the colonies and the mother country. "We can't conceive," he wrote, "that being Americans should deprive us of the benefits of British subjects." In 1758 he did, finally, resign.

Each rebuff had brought Washington closer to his own Virginia troops. His craving for British recognition was replaced by "the hope of meriting the love of my country [Virginia] and the friendly regard of my acquaintances." Washington still wanted the prestige and glory of a military command, but he came to see a special significance in a command of his fellow citizens, of Americans.

In 1772 Washington had been a civilian for fourteen years, enjoying the benefits of his landed estates. The Stamp Act and the Townshend Acts had already provoked revolutionary stirrings in the colonies; the Virginia House of Burgesses had voted to support the Sons of Liberty in Massachusetts; the Boston Massacre was two years old. And, in posing for his first portrait, George Washington chose to wear the uniform of the military service from which he had retired in 1758—the Virginia Regiment, troops of an American line. It was, for the British, a small but ominous gesture.

The exhibition also includes:

Letter from George Washington to Richard Washington in England, December 6, 1755. George Washington ordered *Sundry Goods* necessary to outfit himself properly for the trip he made to Boston seeking *preferment in a military way*. *Lent by the Library of Congress.*

Letter to George Washington from Captain Robert Orme, November 10, 1755. Orme advised that if Washington failed to obtain a commission in the British Army he should resign from military service altogether because *Mount Vernon would offered* [sic] *you more happiness.*
Lent by the Library of Congress.

THE STAGE

For what with my own business, my present Wards, my Mother's . . . Colonel Colville's, Mrs. Savage's, Colonel Fairfax's, Colonel Mercer's . . . and the little assistance I have undertaken to give in the management of my brother Augustine's affairs . . . keeps me, together with the share I take in public affairs, constantly engaged in writing letters, settling accounts, and negotiating one piece of business or another in behalf of one or [an]other of these concerns.
—George Washington to John West
January 13, 1775

As a Virginia gentleman, George Washington was expected to act a role that would distinguish him as belonging to the genteel order and to surround himself with the symbols of gentility.

A gentleman owned land, and a great gentleman controlled vast expanses of land. A gentleman was distinguishable by his personal and public style. A gentleman was marked by his assumption of particular private and civic duties.

George Washington was careful to manifest the proper symbols of a Virginia squire. He took care to perform the parts assigned to him. Without an accepted presence, without a proper performance, he could neither respect himself nor command the respect of other colonial gentlemen. Washington moved upon the stage that was colonial Virginia, meticulously accumulating his accoutrements and props, and steadfastly playing his role.

THE LAND: "A MOST PERMANENT ESTATE"

We went through most beautiful Groves of Sugar Trees and spent the best part of the Day in admiring the Trees and richness of the Land.
—George Washington in
Journey Over the Mountains 1747/8

For centuries, land had been scarce in the British Isles because ownership was concentrated among a small number of aristocrats. Possession of large landholdings became a mark of the highest social rank.

To colonial gentlemen mimicking the standards and images of the English gentry, land was the central symbol of membership in their social order as well as the source of their wealth. The possession of land defined a Virginian as a gentleman; it gave to him an aura of authenticity, of accomplishment, of special standing.

Having learned while still in his teens the symbolic value of owning land, George Washington had made his first land purchase at the age of eighteen with money he had saved from surveying jobs. In the years that followed, he increased his holdings by tens of thousands of acres through purchases, military bounty receipts, marriage, speculative schemes, and cooperative ventures with other gentlemen.

Land was crucial to Washington's sense of himself. He purchased landscape paintings and prints to hang on the walls of the public rooms in his home long before it was fashionable to do so, thus surrounding himself in a symbolic mantle of land.

Figure 83
Falls of the Genesee, by William Winstanley.
Oil on canvas, $43\frac{5}{8}''$ by $52\frac{7}{8}''$.
George Washington purchased this landscape in 1794.
From the Lewis Collection,
National Museum of American History.

Figure 84

Walker-Washington Map, George Washington's holographic copy of a map made by Dr. Thomas Walker of the *Aligany*. It seems likely that Washington made this map to use on his *journey to the Ohio* in 1770, one of his many trips into the *uninhabited wilds*.
Lent by the Library of Congress.

The exhibition also includes:

List of Shareholders in the Dismal Swamp Company. Washington had a lifelong interest in land development schemes and he joined with investors in a variety of stock companies.
Lent by the George Washington National Masonic Memorial.

Receipt endorsed by George Washington for money paid to Washer Blunt for work done for the Potomac Company, 1786. Washington joined with neighbors to form a company to bear the expense of clearing the Potomac River and operating a toll waterway to link frontier resources to coastal markets.
Lent by the Mount Vernon Ladies' Association.

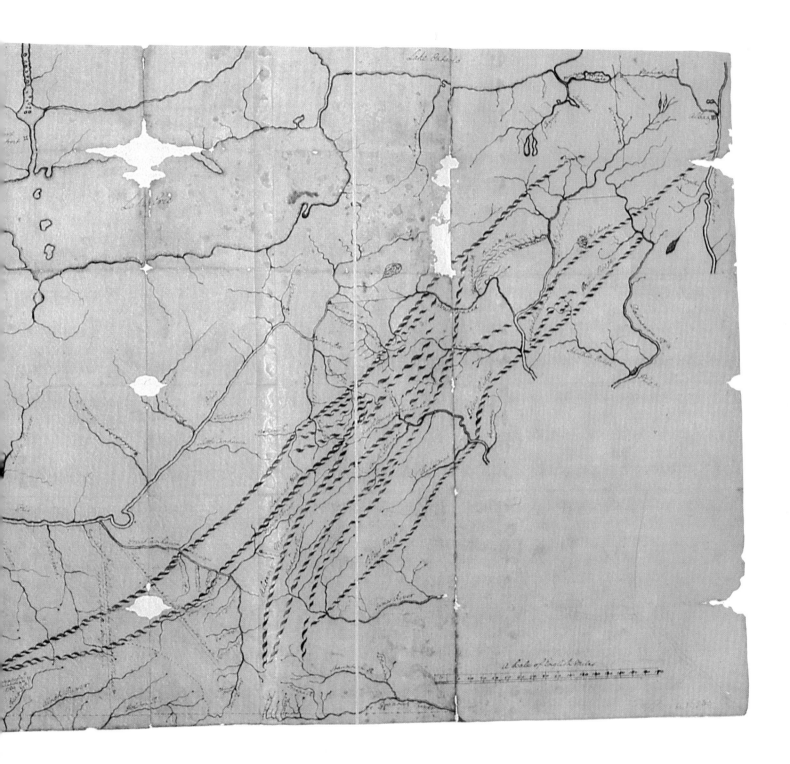

Lake Ontario

a Scale of English Miles

THE MOUNT VERNON FAMILY: "DOMESTIC FELICITY"

I am now I believe fixed at this Seat with an agreeable Consort for Life and hope to find more happiness in retirement than I ever experienc'd amidst a wide and bustling World.
—George Washington to Richard Washington
September 20, 1759

Portrait of Martha Dandridge Custis, by Ernest Fisher, about 1850, after the original by John Wollaston.
Oil on canvas, 49½" × 40½".
Lent by The White House.

Figure 85
On exhibit by special courtesy of Washington and Lee University, Lexington, Virginia, during June and July 1982:
The original portrait of Martha Dandridge Custis, by John Wollaston, 1757.
Oil on canvas, 50" × 41".

Figure 86
Iron treasure chest belonging to Martha Washington's first husband, Daniel Parke Custis. She inherited the chest and his estate upon his death.
Lent by the Mount Vernon Ladies' Association.

The exhibition also includes:

Polychrome Chinese export porcelain bowl. The style of this piece of Mount Vernon china pre-dates Washington's marriage and thus may have belonged to Martha Dandridge Custis before her marriage to George Washington.
From the Lewis Collection,
National Museum of American History.

George Washington had long sought his agreeable consort. Together with the church and the civil government, the family unit provided the primary framework around which people in colonial Virginia organized their lives. It was therefore important for a gentleman to choose a suitable wife.

Washington's search for a wife began in earnest when he turned twenty. As a teenager his "Poor Resistless Heart" had been undone by a young girl's "bright sparkling Eyes," but as he assumed the more dignified manners of a man he became less concerned with surrendering to "cupids feather'd Dart." Instead, he was interested in finding a woman whose land and wealth could enhance the financial foundations of his life.

Betsy Fauntleroy, the daughter of a wealthy Virginian, was one such woman, but she refused his proposal. Mary Eliza Philipse, heiress of a New York barony, had a dowry which included an inviting 51,000 acres of land, but she looked more favorably on a man nearer home and Washington withdrew his solicitations. Success finally came with Martha Dandridge Custis, a wealthy widow with two small children and a fine fortune as well as a good disposition and good sense. Washington began courting her in the spring of 1758 and in less than a year they were married. Disappointed in his military career, he resolved to settle down at Mount Vernon to the life of a Virginia gentleman.

Washington was never to father any children of his own, but he relished the presence of children. He loved to indulge Martha's two children with treats, and he enjoyed their squealing as they played with their "Tea Sett, Grocer's Shop, Neat dress'd Wax Baby, Smoaking Man, books, and Box of Ginger br'd Toys."

Figure 87
On exhibit by special courtesy of Washington and Lee University, Lexington, Virginia, during June and July 1982:
Original portrait of John Parke (Jacky) Custis and Martha Parke (Patsy) Custis, by John Wollaston, 1757.
Oil on canvas, 49″ × 35″.

The exhibition also includes:

Letter from Martha Washington to Margaret Green, June 26, 1761. From the time she was twelve years old, Patsy Custis suffered from epilepsy. Her mother's letter reflects her concern about Patsy's health and a new treatment being tried.
Lent by the Mount Vernon Ladies' Association.

Letter from George Washington to Jonathan Boucher, May 30, 1768. Washington enrolled Jack, his *Son-in-law and Ward* in Rev. Boucher's school in Annapolis.
Lent by the Historical Society of Pennsylvania.

Letter from John Patterson to George Washington, September 2, 1758. Patterson, who had been hired to supervise the renovations of the house while Washington was away with the army, reports on the progress, or rather the lack of it, in *laying floor . . . Plastering . . . & Paynting.*
Lent by the Library of Congress.

THE LIFESTYLE: "DOMESTIC ENJOYMENTS"

A gentleman and his lady were known by their lifestyle. Washington, sensitive to such appearances, did everything he could to assure that he and Martha presented themselves with the proper trappings.

Prior to his marriage, Washington had the house at Mount Vernon enlarged and made more stylish. Soon afterwards, he greatly expanded his adjacent properties, making the mansion house into a proper country seat.

Figure 88
Elevation of the west front of Mount Vernon drawn by Washington. Washington, perhaps fancying himself something of an architect, dabbled in designs for renovations of the mansion house.
Lent by the Mount Vernon Ladies' Association.

Once Martha settled herself at Mount Vernon, Washington ordered many luxurious items from England; furniture, rugs, art, china, glass and silver, clothes, fabrics and jewelry, spices, sweetmeats and fine wines, books, toys, and even a parrot for the children were all in keeping with the latest styles. They also had thirteen house slaves and a personal body slave for each child.

The domestic expenditures "swallowed before I knew where I was all the money I got by marriage," wrote Washington, "nay more, brought me into debt." Nevertheless, the way of life to which they both were accustomed and aspired required the outlay.

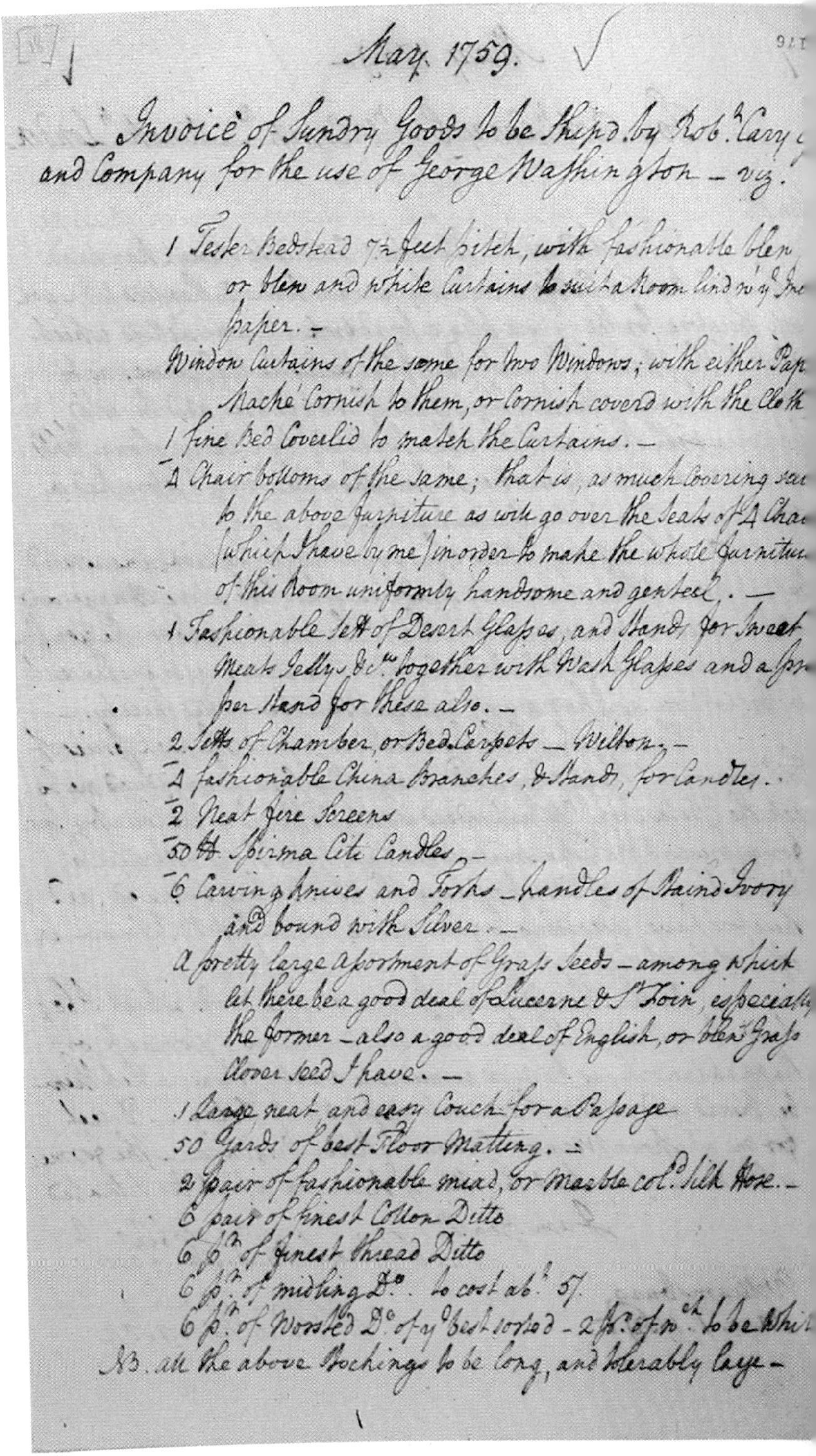

May 1759.

Invoice of Sundry Goods to be Shipd by Robt. Cary and Company for the use of George Washington — viz.

1 Tester Bedstead 7½ feet pitch, with fashionable blew or blew and white Curtains to suit a Room lind w/ ye Ire paper. —

Window Curtains of the same for two Windows; with either Papier Mache Cornish to them, or Cornish coverd with the Cloth

1 fine Bed Coverlid to match the Curtains. —

4 Chair bottoms of the same; that is, as much covering suitable to the above furniture as will go over the Seats of 4 Chairs (which I have by me) in order to make the whole furniture of this Room uniformly handsome and genteel. —

1 Fashionable sett of Desert Glasses, and Stands for Sweet Meats Jellys &c. together with Wash Glasses and a proper Stand for these also. —

2 Setts of Chamber, or Bed Carpets — Wilton. —

4 fashionable China Branches, & Stands, for Candles.

2 Neat fire Screens

50 lb. Spirma Citi Candles. —

6 Carving Knives and Forks — handles of Staind Ivory and bound with Silver. —

A pretty large assortment of Grass Seeds — among which let there be a good deal of Lucerne & St Foin, especially the former — also a good deal of English, or blew Grass Clover seed I have. —

1 Large neat and easy Couch for a Passage

50 Yards of best Floor Matting. —

2 pair of fashionable mixd, or Marble Cold. Silk Hose. —

6 pair of finest Cotton Ditto

6 pr. of finest thread Ditto

6 pr. of midling Do. to cost abt. 5/

6 pr. of Worsted Do. of ye best sorted — 2 pr. of wch. to be Whi

NB. all the above Stockings to be long, and tolerably large —

Figure 89
Letter with invoice from George Washington to *Robert Cary & Company, Merchants, London,* May 1, 1759, in which he orders goods for his new family.
Lent by the Library of Congress.

May 1759. ✓ [19]

Invoice Continued. —

1 piece of finest and most most fashionable Stock Tape
1 Suit of Cloaths of the finest Cloth, & fashionable Colour
    made by the Inclosd measure. —
The newest, and most approvd Treatise of Agriculture — besides
    this send me a small piece in Octavo — calld a New System
    of Agriculture or a Speedy way to grow Rich
Langleys Book of Gardening. —
Gibson upon Horses the latest Edition in Quarto. —
Half a doz. pair of Mens neatest Shoes and Pumps, to be
    made by one Didsbury on Col. Baylors Last — but a little
    larger than his & to have high Heels. —
6 ps. Mens Riding Gloves — rather larger than the middle size —
One neat Pocket Book capable of receiving Memorandums &
    small Cash acct to be made of Ivory, or any thing else that
    will admit of cleaning. —
Fine soft Calf Skin for a pair of Boots — her leathr. for Soles. —
Six Bottles of Greenhows Tincture
Order from the best House in Madeira a Pipe of the best old Wine,
and let it be Secured from Pilferers. —

                                  Go: Washington
Will m. 8 May 1759 —   (465)

The exhibition also includes:

Marble-top table used at Mount Vernon.
Washington did buy locally-made items like this
table when they were available. The style of the
table suggests that it was acquired for the house
about the time of the Washington's marriage.
From the Lewis Collection,
National Museum of American History.

Chippendale ladder-back side chair. When Martha
Washington returned to Mount Vernon at the end
of the war in 1783, she went by way of Philadelphia
to procure some Articles of Furniture and stores which
General Washington said were *for my home
in Virginia.*
From the Peter Collection,
National Museum of American History.

Fire screen ordered from England, c.1760. In the
nineteenth century, the screen was covered with a
portion of a dress worn by Martha Washington.
From the Peter Collection,
National Museum of American History.

Three silver-handle knives and four forks. An
invoice of August 20, 1757, records the shipment
from London of *2 Setts best Silver handle Knives &
Forks best. London Blades £11-0-0, Engraving 53
Crests £1-6-6.*
From the Lewis Collection,
National Museum of American History.

Figure 90

Dining room furnishings used by the Washingtons at Mount Vernon. The blue and white Chinese export porcelain platters and bowl were described by Martha Washington in her Will as *the ware in common use*. The creamware bowl and plate, examples of the *cream-coloured ware* perfected by the Wedgwood Pottery in England in the eighteenth century, appear in Washington's accounts as both *flint* and *Queen's china*. The shagreen (sharkskin) covered knife case is one of several owned by the Washingtons. *From the Lewis Collection, National Museums of American History.*

The exhibition also includes:

American-made bottle chest and bottles. Cases to hold bottles of wine and spirits were commonplace in eighteenth century households. This case, which held nine gallon bottles, was part of the furnishings at Mount Vernon.
From the Peter Collection,
National Museum of American History.

Mirror with black and gold cglomisc pancl, originally part of a dressing table used at Mount Vernon. The mirror would have been recessed into the table and pulled up by the ring at the top when the table was in use.
From the Lewis Collection,
National Museum of American History.

Figure 91
Tea box with mother-of-pearl inlay owned by the Washingtons.
From the Lewis Collection,
National Museum of American History.

George Washington appreciated the importance of personal appearance as a symbol of his various roles in society and took pains to dress appropriately. As a Virginia gentleman, he attired himself "in genteel Dress," wearing "plain Cloathes" with "neither Lace nor Embroidery." As a soldier, he ordered proper uniforms for himself and his troops, concerning himself with buttons, trimmings, and all manner of details. For his inauguration as President, he sought a suit of American-manufactured cloth, one elegant yet free of the "follies of luxury and ostentation." Washington's careful attention to the details of his wardrobe and that of his family continued throughout his life.

Figure 92
Gold watch with extra case given to Martha Washington by her husband. The watchworks bear the mark, *Rd. Webster Exchange Alley 3175,* identifying London clockmaker Richard Webster, 1784-1840.
From the Peter Collection, National Museum of American History.

Figure 93
Account Book kept by William Carlin, a tailor who worked in Alexandria, Virginia. Washington supplemented his imported attire with things which could be made close to home, assuring a better fit and a selection of fabric and style.
Lent by Mrs. Russell R. Taylor.

The exhibition also includes:

Amber necklace owned by Martha Washington. Martha's fondness for jewelry is reflected in George Washington's account books, which show entries for the purchase of jewelry during all the years of their marriage.
National Museum of American History.

Corset with baleen boning owned by Martha Washington, American, 18th century.
From the Peter Collection,
National Museum of American History.

Silk-knit breeches owned by George Washington, probably English, c.1760. George Washington included requests for silk-knit breeches in his orders to England in the 1760s and 1770s. For a pair of black silk-knit breeches ordered in 1767 he specified, . . . *let the Breeches have cool lining fit for Summer wear and a side pocket.*
From the Lewis Collection,
National Museum of American History.

Twill-weave woolen waistcoat owned by George Washington, 1785-88. The diamond-shape embroidery design used to decorate the edges is formed of one blue silk thread and one silver-wrapped yellow silk thread. A small silver paillette was centered in each diamond.
From the Lewis Collection,
National Museum of American History.

Gloves worn by George Washington.
Lent by the Mount Vernon Ladies' Association.

Powder bag and puff owned by George Washington. While Washington never wore a wig, he did conform to the male fashion of the eighteenth century by powdering his chestnut-red hair for formal occasions.
Lent by the Mount Vernon Ladies' Association.

Washington and his wife enjoyed sharing their gracious life at Mount Vernon with their friends. The mansion house was constantly filled with guests, and they were well-known for their hospitality. Visitors from far and near joined them for the gentry's favored recreations—dining, fox hunting, card playing, evenings of music, and dancing (which Washington "relished").

Almost every entry in Washington's diary records the people who came and went, and those whom Washington and his family visited in return. Theirs was a close-knit circle of fashionable friends which extended throughout the Chesapeake-Tidewater region.

Figure 94
Brass hunting horn used at Mount Vernon.
Lent by the Mount Vernon Ladies' Association.

Figure 95
Sheet music of *Two Grand Sonatas for Clavichord or Pianoforte*, composed by *Mr. Pleyel, London*, which belonged to Martha Parke Custis, Martha's granddaughter. A visitor to Mount Vernon wrote that he had been *much Charmed* by *Miss Custis's . . . vocal and instrumental music.*
From the Peter Collection,
National Museum of American History.

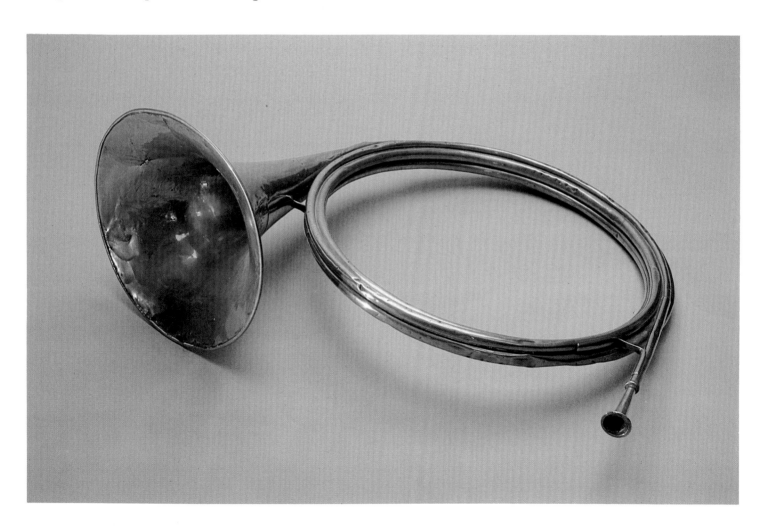

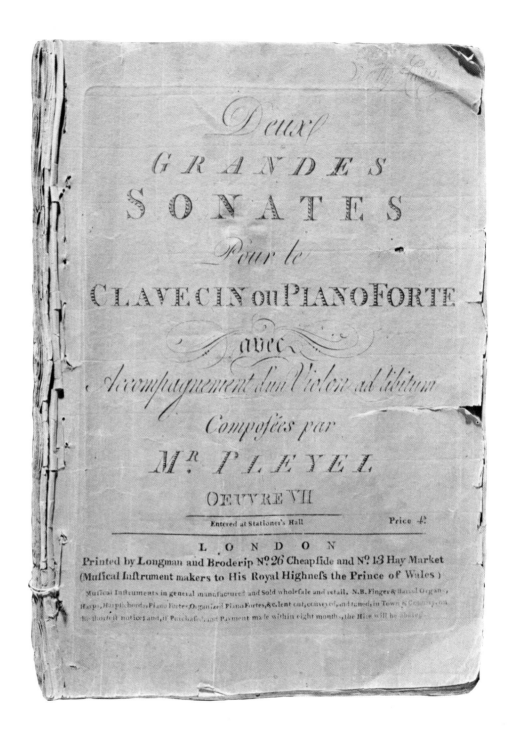

Deux

GRANDES
SONATES

Pour le

CLAVECIN ou PIANOFORTE

avec

Accompagnement d'un Violon ad libitum

Composées par

Mr. PLEYEL

OEUVRE VII

Entered at Stationer's Hall   Price 4ˢ

LONDON

Printed by Longman and Broderip Nº 26 Cheapside and Nº 13 Hay Market
(Musical Instrument makers to His Royal Highness the Prince of Wales)

Musical Instruments in general manufactured and Sold wholesale and retail. N.B. Finger & Barrel Organs,
Harps, Harpsichords, Piano Fortes, Organized Piano Fortes, &c. lent out, conveyed, and tuned, in Town & Country, on
the shortest notice; and, if Purchased, and Payment made within eight months, the Hire will be abated.

1772						
Feby	28	To Cash lost at Fredericksburg	3		2	
Mar.	9	To Ditto lost in Williamsburg	3			
	13	To Ditto lost in Ditto	3		1	
	16	To Ditto Ditto	3		3	
	17	To Ditto Ditto	4			
	21	To Ditto Ditto	4		6	
		Ditto Ditto	4		1	17
	24	To Ditto Ditto	4		6	5
	28	To Ditto Ditto	4		6	
April	1	To Ditto Ditto	4		5	
	2	To Ditto Ditto	4		1	5
	6	To Ditto Ditto	4		1	
	7	To Ditto Ditto	5		7	
	12	To Ditto in Fredericksburg	50		1	
June	2	To Ditto in Frederick	50			8
	15	To Ditto at Home	55			8
July	2	To Ditto at Ditto	55		1	10
	15	To Ditto at Do	55		1	10
	27	To Ditto at Do	55		1	5
Augt	20	To Ditto in Alexandria	60		1	5
Septr	16	To Ditto in Fredericksburg	60		2	0
	30	To Ditto at Home	61		1	0
Novr	13	To Ditto in Williamsburg	62			12
Decr	12	To Ditto at Home	63			8
1773		To Ditto at Ditto	82		3	10
Mar	13	To Ditto at Ditto	88		1	10
	27	To Ditto at Ditto	88			7
April	24	To Ditto at Home	91		3	4
Augt	31	To Ditto Ditto	93		3	13
Septr	1	To Ditto at Annapolis	96		3	1
Decr	31	To Ditto in Williamsburg	98			16
1774		To Ditto Do	105			10
May	16	To Ditto Williamsburg	110			15
	18	To Ditto Ditto	112		2	10
June	10	To Ditto Ditto	112		5	15
				£	78	5

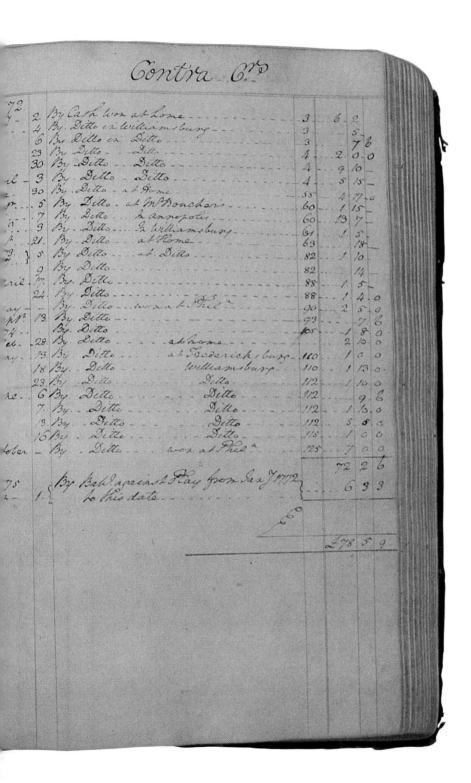

Figure 96
George Washington's Account Book for 1772-1793,
showing money won and lost at *cards & other Play*.
Lent by the Library of Congress.

The exhibition also includes:

George Washington's pocket fishing tackle kit.
Lent by the Mount Vernon Ladies' Association.

English/American Flintlock Fowler of the type
Washington might have used, c.1750. Although
most of the fine sporting firearms used by colonial
planters were imported from England, some were
fabricated in the Colonies utilizing imported parts.
This example was made by John Scott in Charleston,
South Carolina.
*From the Charles Bremmer Hogg Jackson Collection,
National Museum of American History.*

Lottery ticket.
Lent by the Mount Vernon Ladies' Association.

Sheet music case owned by the Washingtons.
Martha, her daughter, and granddaughters all
played musical instruments.
*From the Lewis Collection,
National Museum of American History.*

*The Bull Finch, Being A Choice Collection of the
Newest & Most Favorite English Song*, London.
The songbook, which belonged to Martha
Washington, is inscribed with her name.
Lent by the Mount Vernon Ladies' Association.

THE SLAVES: "MY NEGROES"

The "uniformly handsome and genteel" stage settings for the luxurious and leisurely life at Mount Vernon were supported by a network of slavery. Washington's country seat was the locale of many enjoyments, but it was also a working plantation which required vast quantities of semi-skilled and unskilled labor to function properly.

Slavery was an unquestioned institution throughout most of Virginia; Washington himself had inherited slaves at the age of eleven. The comfortable lives of gentlemen like Washington were dependent on the labor and services of enslaved blacks. And owning many slaves, like presiding over many acres of land, was to some degree symbolic of a gentleman's place in the gentry.

The exhibition also includes:

Cherry cricket (footstool).
From the Lewis Collection,
National Museum of American History.

Kitchen table.
Lent by the Mount Vernon Ladies' Association.

Windsor chair.
Lent by the Mount Vernon Ladies' Association.

Housekeeping equipment used at Mount Vernon: preserve jar of Wagstaff-Vauxhall pottery, coffee mill, copper egg poacher, copper kettle lid, tin warmer, tin cannister, copper preserving kettle, pewter plate warmer, pewter platter, iron pot stand, iron pot hook, quilting frame, and fire bellows.
From the Peter Collection,
National Museum of American History.

Figure 97
Tin warmer, coffee mill, and copper egg
poacher used in the kitchen at Mount Vernon.
*From the Peter Collection,
National Museum of American History.*

Washington considered slaves "a Species of property" like farming equipment, livestock, or the land itself. In fact, he was rather less fond of his slaves than he was of his "Breeding Mares or Stock of other kinds." Nonetheless, Washington was well-known for his benevolent treatment of his slaves. They were properly fed and clothed, and doctors were regularly called to his various plantations to care for them.

Such care was partly practical; Washington viewed mistreating or neglecting slaves so badly that they died as "incurring an expense for nothing." Yet Washington was motivated by more than a desire to minimize his losses. He believed that his slaves were like children, unable to care for themselves without the oversight of a father-figure. Like most of his contemporaries, he did not recognize the sophisticated social structures rooted in their African traditions or the psychological defenses that enabled them to maintain their integrity as an inner-directed people even in slavery.

Washington believed that he was under an obligation to provide his slaves with proper care, protection, and guidance. He often chastised his overseers for treating them like "brute beasts." Indeed, the proper execution of this self-imposed, honor-borne responsibility to his slaves was important to Washington's self-image and self-respect as a gentleman.

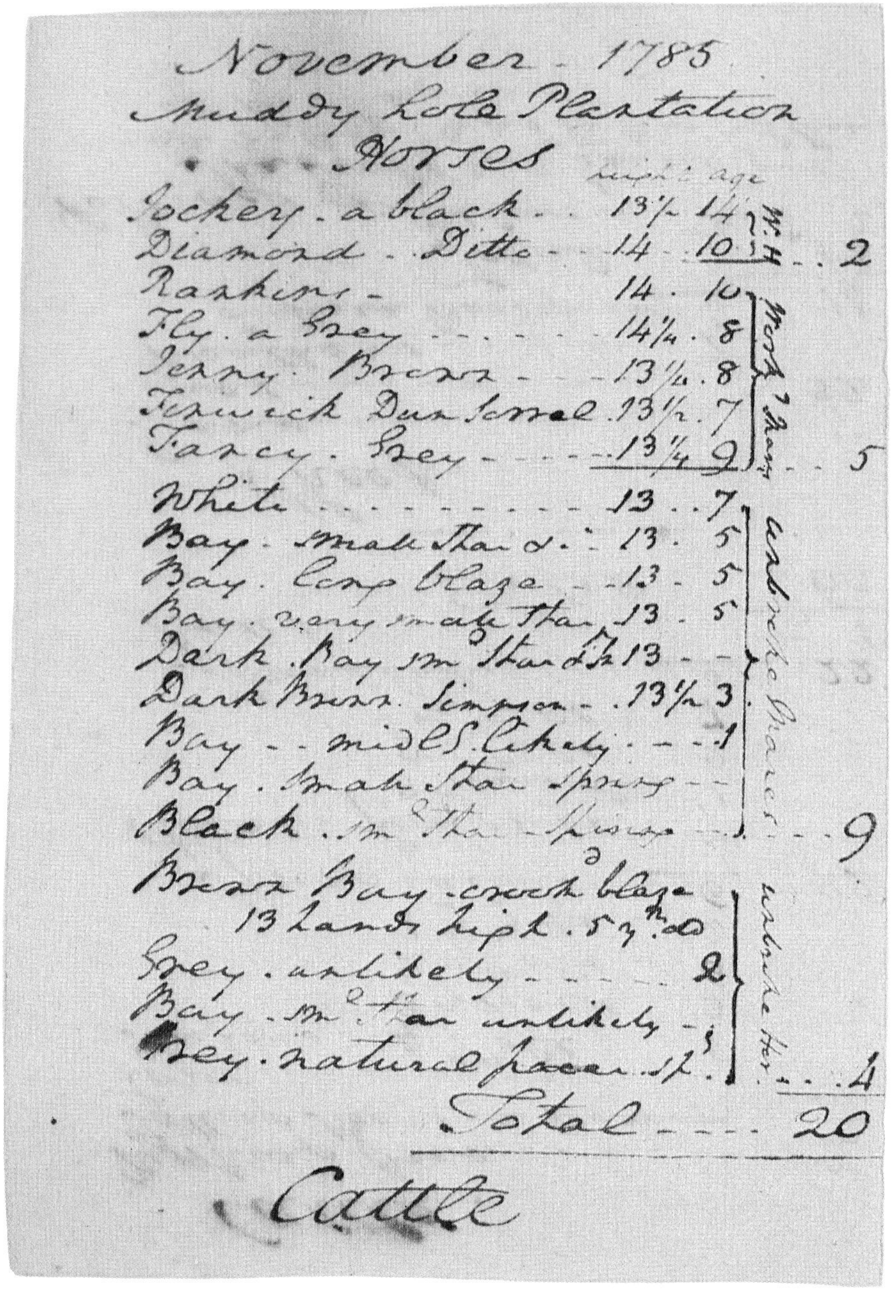
November – 1785.
Muddy hole Plantation
Horses — height age
Jockey – a black – 13½ 14 } W.H.
Diamond – Ditto – 14 – 10 } . . 2
Rankins – 14 . 10
Fly – a Grey – 14¼ . 8
Jenny – Brown – 13½ . 8
Fenwick Dun Sorrel 13½ . 7
Fancy – Grey – 13¼ 9 } Work Horses . . 5
White – 13 . 7
Bay – small Star &c – 13 . 5
Bay – long blaze – 13 . 5
Bay – very small Star 13 . 5
Dark Bay sm Star & Sn 13 – –
Dark Brown Simpson – 13½ 3
Bay – midl. likely – – 1
Bay – Small Star Spring – –
Black – sm Star – Spring – } unbroke Mares . . 9
Brown Bay – crooked blaze 13 hands high . 5 yrs old
Grey – unlikely – 2
Bay – sm Star unlikely
Grey – natural pacer } unbroke Hor. . . 4
Total . . . 20
Cattle

Figure 98
Listing of stock from George Washington's *Diary*, November 15, 1785. *Went to my Neck Plantation and compleated the Acct. of my Stock there—except that of the Hogs—which stands thus. Lent by the Library of Congress.*

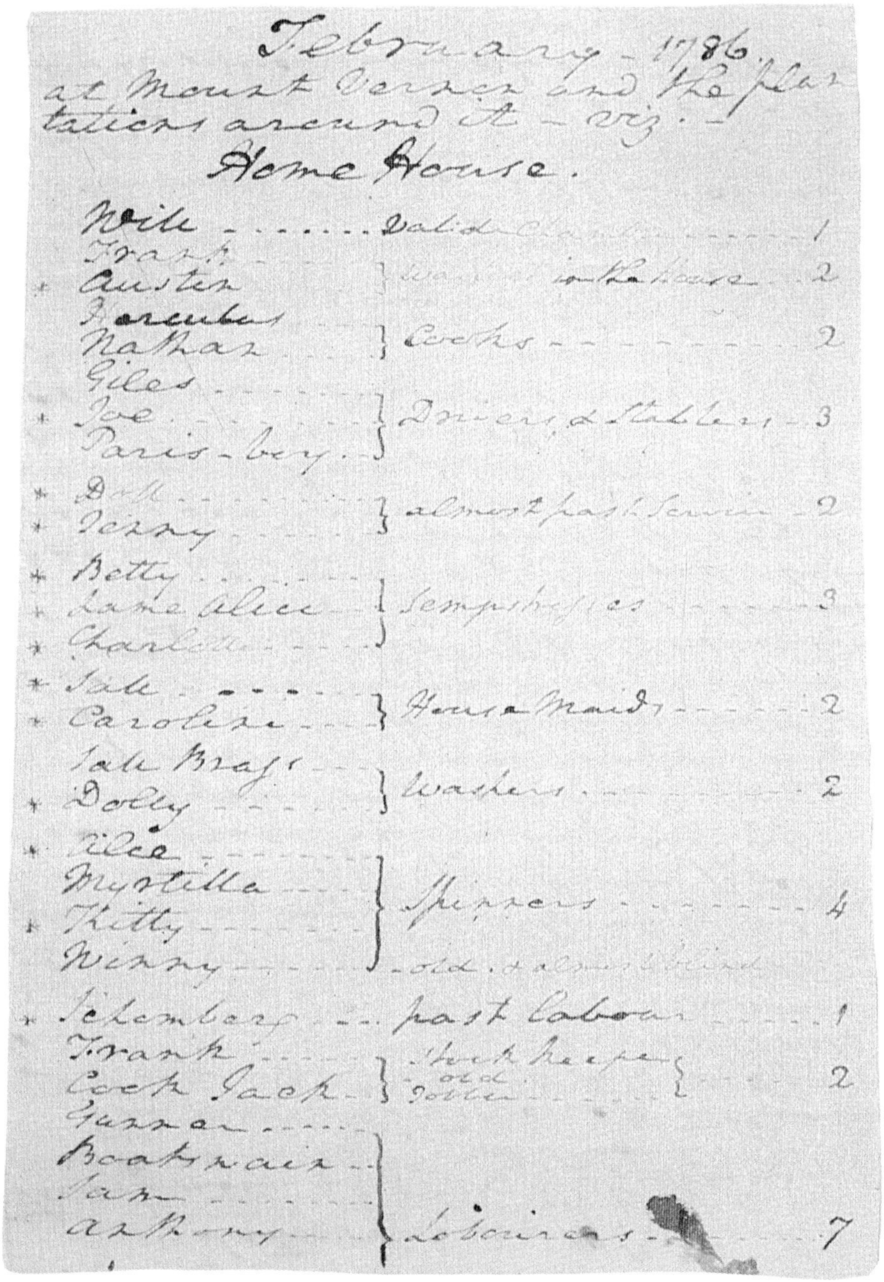

February—1786.
at Mount Vernon and the plantations around it—viz.—
Home House.

Will .... Val de Chambre 1
Frank, Austin } Waiters in the house 2
Hercules, Nathan } Cooks 2
Giles, Joe, Paris—boy } Drivers & Stablers 3
Doll, Jenny } almost past Service 2
Betty, Lame Alice, Charlotte } Sempstresses 3
Sall, Caroline } House Maids 2
Sall Brass, Dolly } Washers 2
Alce, Myrtilla, Kitty } Spinners 4
Winny .... old & almost blind
Schomberg .... past labour 1
Frank, Cook Jack } Stock keeper, old fellow } 2
Gunner, Boatswain, Sam, Anthony } Labourers 7

Figure 99
Listing of slaves from George Washington's *Diary*, February 18, 1786. *Took a list to day of all my Negroes which are as follows at Mount Vernon and the plantations around it.*
Lent by the Library of Congress.

The exhibition also includes:

An overseer doing his duty, sketched from life near Fredericsburg [Virginia], by Benjamin Henry Latrobe, March 13, 1798. Pencil, pen and ink and watercolor on paper.
Lent by the Maryland Historical Society, Papers of Benjamin Henry Latrobe.

Letter from George Washington to William Pearce, May 10, 1795, instructing him in ways to deal with particular slaves and problems pertaining to the management of his plantations.
Lent by the Mount Vernon Ladies' Association.

Washington's slave holdings represented not merely a large initial expenditure, but also a huge continuing investment in food, clothing, and medical care. Through procreation, his force of slave labor became so large that the cost of maintaining it exceeded the value of its labor, particularly as Washington diverted parcels of his land from tobacco to less labor-intensive crops. Many of his fellow planters sold off their surplus slaves. Washington, however, hoped for an act of the Legislature that would, by abolishing slavery, free him of his responsibilities to them and, at the same time, compensate him for the property so lost.

In the face of Washington's reluctance to sell his surplus slaves, his need to defray his expenses led him to advertise for rent portions of his land to farmers of "good reputation" who also would pay for the use of the slaves who normally worked those portions of land. No one, however, replied to his newspaper advertisements.

Washington was finally able to resolve the economic problem of his slave-holding by his death. His Will stipulated that after the death of Martha all the slaves he owned were to be freed from the estate. In this way, the monetary investment that the slaves represented would be lost with minimal economic damage to the family.

Even in the end Washington was not able to bring himself to abandon his sense of obligation to his slaves. By his Will a "regular and permanent fund" was established for their support. The executor's account book shows that the estate paid for the livelihood of his former slaves well into the mid-1800s.

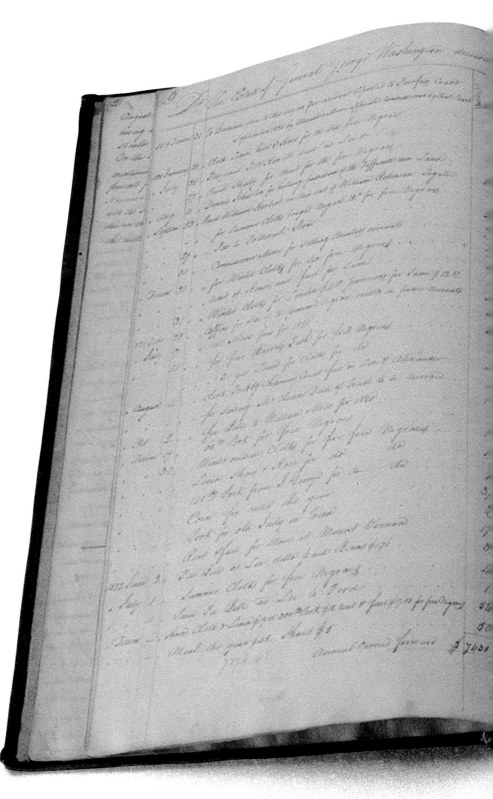

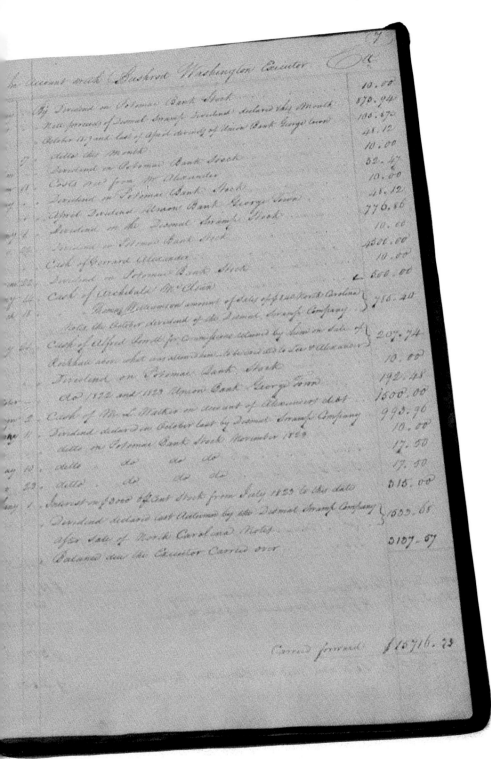

Figure 100
Executor's Account Book kept by *A. Moore, Auditor*, a clerk engaged by Washington's executors to balance the accounts of his estate, showing the variety of disbursements made by Washington's estate to the *free negroes* between 1819 and 1822.
Lent by the Mount Vernon Ladies' Association.

The exhibition also includes:

Bill of sale for three slaves in Fayette County, Pennsylvania, October 21, 1786. Washington did not think that *slaves who are happy and contented with their present masters* should be *tampered with or seduced to leave them.* When the General Assembly of Pennsylvania passed an act that provided for the emancipation of every *Negro and mulatto child,* Washington, fearing that his slaves working his land in the state might *attempt their freedom or become distainful of their enslavement,* ordered his agent Thomas Freeman to sell his property and slaves.
National Museum of American History.

Letter from George Washington to Lawrence Lewis, August 4, 1797, in which he reveals his fears that increasing abolitionist agitation among private humanitarian groups would cause his slaves to *attempt their freedom.*
Lent by the Mount Vernon Ladies' Association.

Census of *Negroes belonging to George Washington in his own right and by Marriage,* June 1799. Three hundred and seventeen slaves lived and worked on Washington's five Tidewater farms.
Lent by the Mount Vernon Ladies' Association.

THE FARMING: "THE LIFE OF A HUSBANDMAN"

The more I am acquainted with agricultural affairs, the better I am pleased with them; insomuch, that I can no where find so great satisfaction as in those innocent and useful pursuits. In indulging these feelings, I am let to reflect how much more delightful to an undebauched mind is the task of making improvements on the earth, than all the vain glory which can be acquired from ravaging it, by the most uninterrupted career of conquests.

—George Washington to Arthur Young
December 4, 1788

Washington was—before, during, and after everything else—a farmer. His diaries and letters show a continuing concern with farming and personal involvement in the management of a plantation community that was in many ways self-supporting. He was constantly occupied with "posting his books" and sending his cash crops into fluctuating markets, making sure of generating enough income to purchase from others goods which could not be produced at Mount Vernon; with keeping track of his livestock—of horses bred, of sheep shorn, of hogs and cattle "killd and dressd"; with arranging for the maintenance of his farms and buildings; and with worrying about the weather and its impact on his plantations.

Washington delighted in both the concerns and pleasures of farming; for him "the life of a Husbandman of all others is the most delectable."

Figure 101
Reproduction of a map of Mount Vernon and Washington's surrounding farms, drawn by Washington in 1793.
Reproduced from the Collections of the Huntington Library.

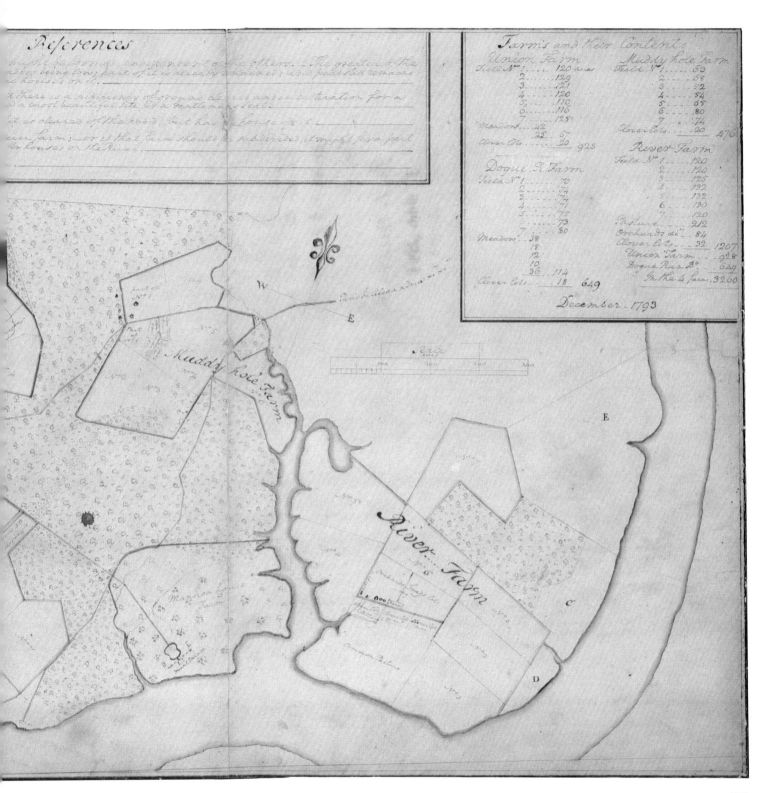

Figure 102
Washington's own copy of *The Gentleman Farmer.*
Being an Attempt to Improve Agriculture by
Subjecting It to the Test of Rational Principles,
by Henry Home, 1779.
Lent by the Boston Athenaeum.

THE

Gentleman Farmer.

BEING

AN ATTEMPT TO IMPROVE

AGRICULTURE,

By subjecting it to the Test

OF

RATIONAL PRINCIPLES.

Semper ego auditor tantum?
Juv.

DUBLIN:

PRINTED BY JAMES WILLIAMS, SKINNER-ROW.

M, DCC, LXXIX.

Shortly after he inherited Mount Vernon, Washington wrote to his London agent asking for a copy of the book "A New System of Agriculture: Or a Speedy Method of Growing Rich." As it turned out, farming did not make Washington rich, a fact in part attributable to his persistent search for a "new" system of agriculture. His continuing experiments focused on different fertilizers and soil conditioners, improved breeds of livestock, innovative agricultural implements, and adaptation of new plant varieties. His goal was to bring permanence to agriculture at Mount Vernon, in contrast to the profligate colonial tradition of farming until the land wore out, then moving on. Many of his experiments failed, while others succeeded in physical but not economic terms.

During the eighteenth century, English agricultural writers espoused a number of non-traditional practices known collectively as "the new husbandry." There were two branches of thought in this school: one, represented by Jethro Tull, believed that plants grew best if the earth was broken into small particles, and advised cultivating with horsedrawn implements. The other, represented by Arthur Young, believed that soil chemistry was the critical element in making plants flourish, and advised crop rotation and soil preparation. Washington owned Tull's book, as well as others that presented new ideas on soil, fertilizers, plant physiology, livestock, and equipment, and corresponded with Young for thirteen years.

Figure 103
Plate from *Horse-Hoeing Husbandry*, by
Jethro Tull, 1731.
National Museum of American History.

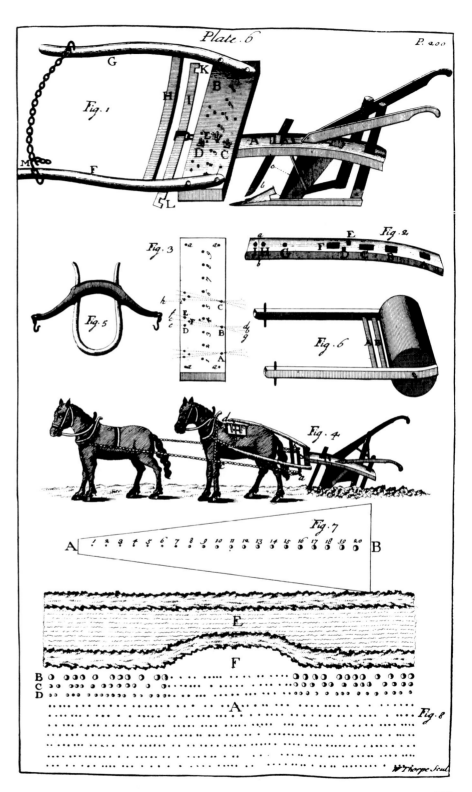

The exhibition also includes:

Certificate of Membership in the Board of
Agriculture, London, 1795. So avid was
Washington's interest in the *new husbandry* that he
was made a member of this board.
Lent by the Library of Congress.

In 1785 Washington built a large greenhouse with a forced-hot-air heating system on the north side of his flower garden at the Mansion House. In this pleasure garden, he raised oranges, pineapples, palm trees, strawberries, and other exotic plants.

The exhibition also includes:

Potted orange tree and box bushes of the varieties George Washington cultivated in his greenhouse; watering can and bell jar used for plant propagation at Mount Vernon.
Lent by the Mount Vernon Ladies' Association.

Hot House Gardener, by John Abercrombie, 1789.
Lent by National Agricultural Library.

Figure 104
Washington's plan for his greenhouse, 1784.
Lent by the Mount Vernon Ladies' Association.

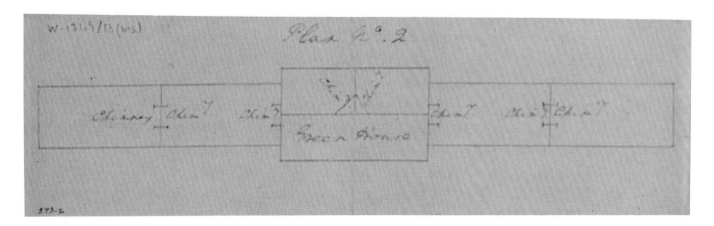

Figure 105
Potted sago palm descended from the original
tree in George Washington's greenhouse.
Lent by the Mount Vernon Ladies' Association.

Washington struggled persistently to achieve control over the environmental and cultural variables that might lead to improved agricultural production. He experimented with over sixty field crops during his farming career, and gradually transferred most of his cultivated land from tobacco to grains.

The exhibition also includes:

Eighteenth century wooden grain shovel.
Lent by Colonial Williamsburg.

Cradle scythe, grain riddle and flail.
National Museum of American History.

Field roller, the only surviving field implement used at Mount Vernon during George Washington's time.
Lent by the Mount Vernon Ladies' Association.

Washington's own copy of *The Young Mill Wright's and Miller's Guide,* by Oliver Evans, 1795. Washington cultivated 700 acres of wheat at his different farms. Recognizing the advantages of milling it himself and selling the flour, he built a grist mill on his property.
Lent by the Boston Athenaeum.

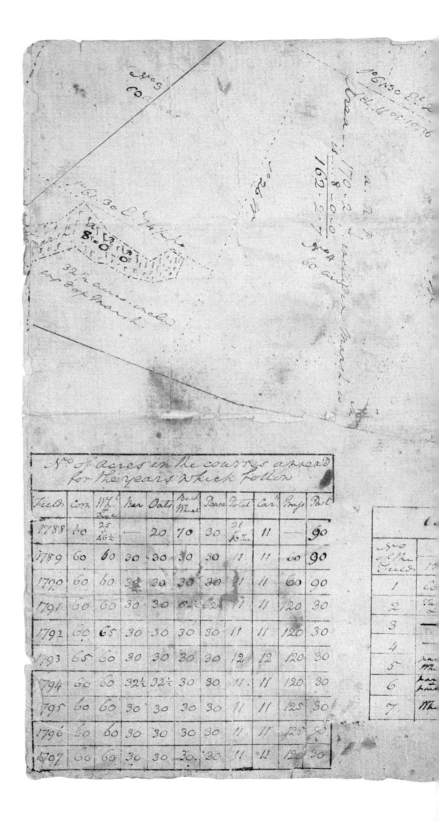

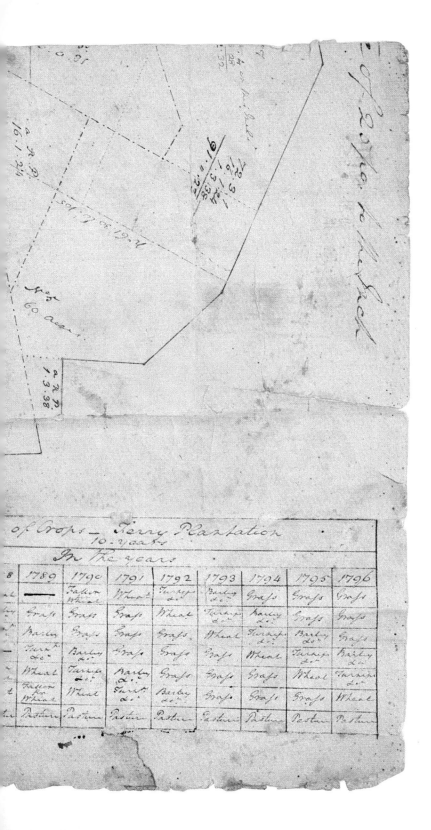

Figure 106
Crop Rotation Series for Ferry Farm. Washington knew that crop rotation had several benefits, including higher yields, lower incidence of weeds, and less soil erosion.
Lent by the Mount Vernon Ladies' Association.

THE PUBLIC DUTIES: "THE PARTS ASSIGNED TO US"

A colonial gentleman was known by his willingness to undertakte civic duties. In Washington's case, sense of responsibility often took precedence over personal enjoyment.

One of the obligations of the Virginia gentry was political leadership, the representation of neighborhood interests at the seat of government. George Washington first ran for the Virginia House of Burgesses from the Winchester area. Defeated in 1755, he won a resounding victory in 1758. As soon as the opportunity presented itself, however, he changed his constituency to Fairfax County, a seat he held until the House was dismissed by the Governor of Virginia at the beginning of the Revolutionary War. Washington also acted as a trustee of the town of Alexandria and served as a justice on the County Court.

A Copy of the Poll taken at an Election of Burgesses for Fairfax County the 16th of July 1765 — and Candidates Names. —

	George Washington		John West		John Posey	
A	Robert Alexander	5	Robert Alexander	5		
	Bryan Allison	T			Bryan Allison	T
	Benjamin Adams	T			Benjamin Adams	T
	Butler Ashford	T	Butler Ashford	T		
	John Anderson	5	John Anderson			
	Richard Arrol	F	Richard Arrol			
	John Alexander Senr	F			John Alexander Senr	
	Philip Alexander	F	Philip Alexander	5		
	James Adams	F	James Adams			
			Michael Ashford		Michael Ashford	
			John Askins		John Askin	5
			Silvester Adams		Silvester Adams	
			William Adams	10		
			Charles Alexander		Charles Alexander	
			Thomas Asbury			
B	Henry Boggess	T			Henry Boggess	
	Marmaduke Beckwith	T			Marmaduke Beckwith	
	Samuel Berkley	T			Samuel Berkley	12
	William Barker	T			William Barker	
	William Boylston	F	William Boylston			
	William Bronaugh	15			William Bronaugh	
	Owen Brady		Owen Brady			
	Thomas Baylis	T			Thomas Baylis	
	John Bronaugh	T			John Bronaugh	
	John Bowling		John Bowling	15		
	John Bah	20	John Bah			
	John Barrey				John Barry	15
	Joseph Bennett				Joseph Bennet	
	Benjn Berkley				Benjn Berkley	
	Abraham Barnes				Abraham Barnes	
	Charles Broadwater	25	Charles Broadwater			
			William Berk		William Berk	
			John Branner			
			Thomas Beach	20	Thomas Beach	20
			Moses Bah			
			Francis Bellenger			
			Gerrard Bowling		Gerrard Bowling	
			Edward Blackburn		Edward Blackburn	

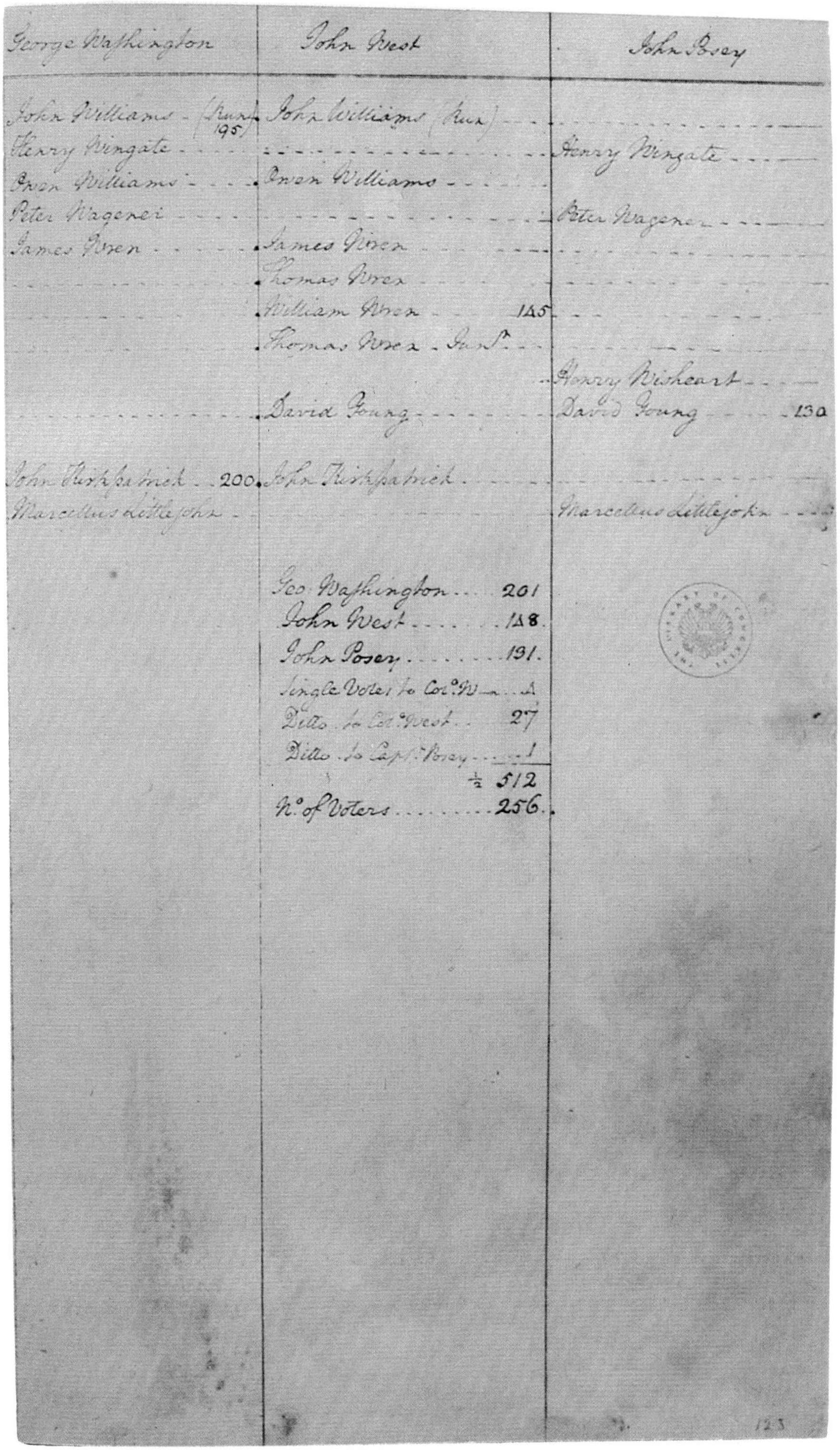

George Washington | John West | John Posey

George Washington	John West	John Posey
John Williams (Henry) 95	John Williams (Hen)	
Henry Wingate		Henry Wingate
Owen Williams	Owen Williams	
Peter Wagener		Peter Wagener
James Posen	James Posen	
	Thomas Posen	
	William Posen 145	
	Thomas Posen Jun.	
		Henry Wisheart
	David Young	David Young 130
John Kirkpatrick 200	John Kirkpatrick	
Marcellus Littlejohn		Marcellus Littlejohn

Geo Washington 201
John West ...... 148.
John Posey ...... 131.
Single Voters to Col:o W .... A
Ditto to Col: West . 27
Ditto to Capt Posey 1
½ 512
No. of Voters .... 256.

Figure 107
A Copy of the Poll Taken at an Election of Burgesses for Fairfax County the 16th of July 1765, which records George Washington's victory.
Lent by the Library of Congress.

The exhibition also includes:

Minute Book of the House of Burgesses, December 5, 1769, showing Washington's appointment to draw a bill for the dredging of the Potomac River. Washington's main interests as a Burgess were matters he considered important to Fairfax County, to his neighbors, and to himself.
Lent by the Viginia State Library.

Watercolor sketch of a townhouse which George Washington owned for use during his frequent business, government, and social visits to Alexandria.
Lent by the George Washington National Masonic Memorial.

County Court Order Book for Fairfax County, Virginia, 1768-1770. The entry of September 21, 1768, records that George Washington took the oath of office according to Law and was sworn in as Justice of the Court.
Lent by the Fairfax County (Virginia) Clerk of the Court.

Washington accepted without question that a man of his social class also had obligations to the Church. He served on the vestry of the Anglican Church and purchased a family pew, although his personal religious life appears to have been more conventional than intense or deep. He said he found "the ways of Providence inscrutable," never doubted Providence's benign nature, and believed that "everything happens for the best."

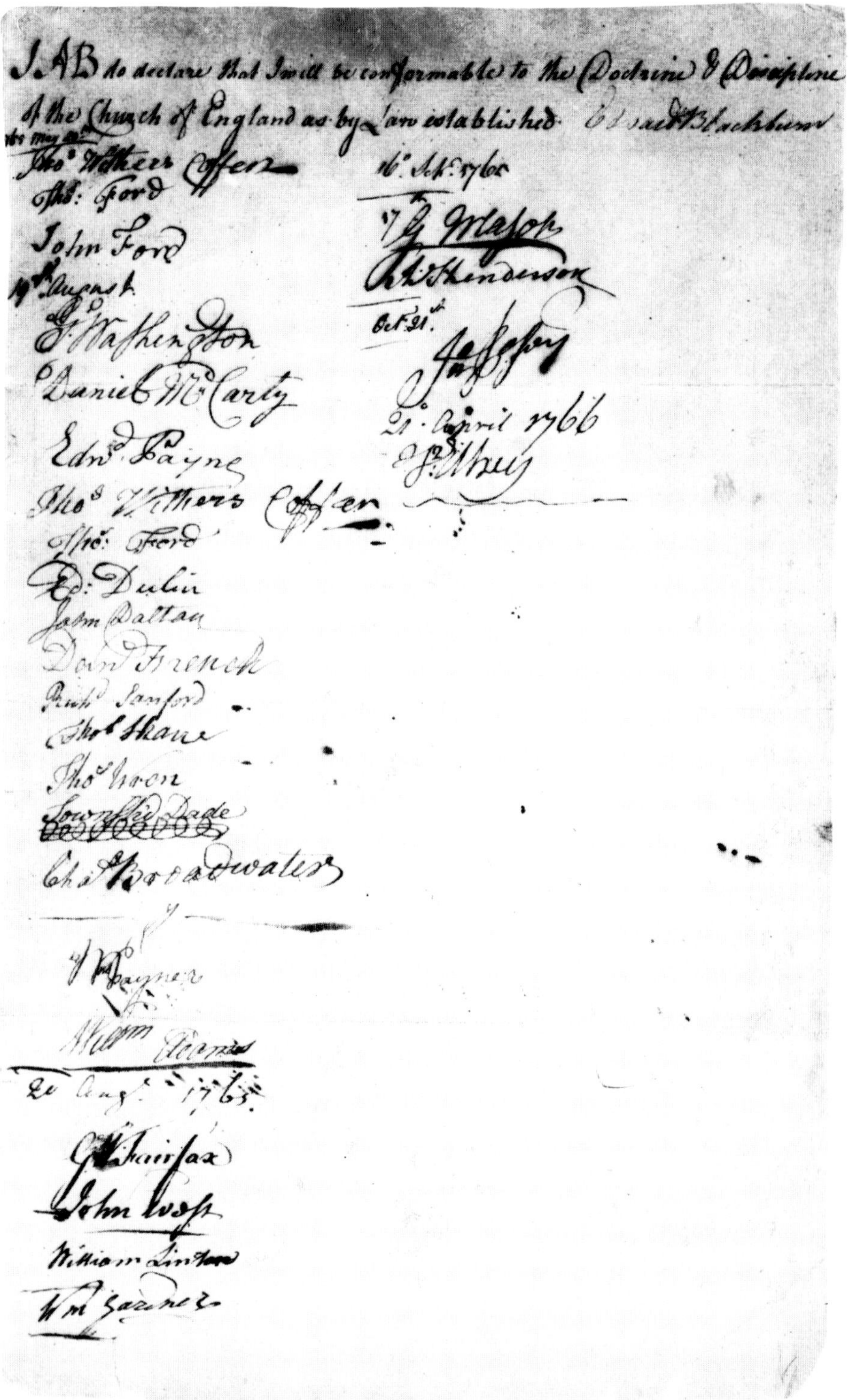
I A B do declare that I will be conformable to the Doctrine & Discipline of the Church of England as by Law established

John Ford

G: Washington

Daniel McCarty

Edwd. Payne

21 April 1766

20 Aug. 1765

John West

Figure 108

Register of Pohick Church, Truro Parish, in which George Washington and other vestrymen signed a declaration, declaring to "be conformable to the Doctrine & Discipline of the Church of England as by Law established."

Lent by The New-York Historical Society.

Washington's initiative in joining the Fredericksburg Lodge of the Masonic Order when he was twenty-one was typical of his peers, socially and politically rather than passionately motivated. The Masonic Order's emphasis on duty, responsibility, order, and reason coincided closely with his own values, however, and the brotherhood with Masons in all parts of Colonial America would prove a valuable asset throughout his life and career.

Figure 109
Silver Masonic jewel owned by George Washington. *Lent by Alexandria-Washington Lodge No. 22, A.F. & A.M.*

The exhibition also includes:

Vestry Book of Truro Parish, Virginia, 1732-1802. The entry for October 25, 1762, records George Washington's election to the vestry. As vestryman he was active in selecting the land for the new church at Pohick.
Lent by Pohick Episcopal Church.

Watercolor of Pohick Church drawn by one of the children of George Mason, c.1840.
Lent by the Board of Regents, Gunston Hall.

Book of Common Prayer owned by Martha Washington.
Lent by the Mount Vernon Ladies' Association.

THE PATERNAL OBLIGATION: "TO ACT A FRIENDLY PART"

Washington served as formal guardian of Martha's two children, but he also undertook many parental responsibilities for his own brothers and for hordes of nieces and nephews. He gave them both advice and material assistance, made possible their schooling, and provided them with work opportunities.

Children were always present at Mount Vernon, even in later years. When Martha's son, Jack Custis, died of camp fever after the Battle of Yorktown, Washington adopted the two youngest Custis children, Nelly and Washington, and brought them to Mount Vernon to become members of the intimate family circle.

The exhibition also includes:

Windsor high chair, a necessary piece of furniture in the household to accommodate the children of family and friends. Tradition identifies this chair as part of the furnishings at Mount Vernon.
Lent by the Mount Vernon Ladies' Association

Figure 110
English guitar given by George Washington to his ward, Nelly Custis. The instrument is stamped with the name of the maker: *Longman & Brodership/No. 26 Cheapside &/No. 18 Haymarket London.* It bears Nelly's initials, *E.P.C.*, in the ivory and on the silver which decorates the guitar.
From the Lewis Collection,
National Museum of American History.

Figure 111
The Washington Family, attributed to Edward Savage, c.1793.
Oil on canvas, 26″ × 36″.
This portrait shows President and Mrs. Washington, their adopted children Eleanor Parke Custis (Nelly) and George Washington Parke Custis (called Washington), and the President's personal slave, Billy Lee.
Lent by National Trust Collection, Woodlawn Plantation.

THE GREAT THEATRE

It was utterly out of my power to refuse this appointment, without exposing my character to such censures, as would have reflected dishonor upon myself, and have given pain to my friends. This, I am sure, could not, and ought not, to be pleasing to you, and must have lessened me considerably in my own esteem.

—George Washington to Martha Washington
June 18, 1775

On the eve of the American Revolution, George Washington had been retired from military service for 23 years. Yet, as Washington played his role upon the stage that was colonial Virginia, he found himself drawn into a larger drama, ready to devote his "Life and Fortune to the cause" by assuming a leading role in preventing "the deprication of American freedom."

Washington's disillusionment with British treatment of American subjects had become so acute that he was once again ready to assume military command, but no longer for reasons of glory and social advancement. The sense of duty he derived from his social class had, during his duty as Colonel in the Virginia Militia, been transformed into a powerful notion of the obligation to serve regardless of benefit and honor. Later, as he practiced the role of the public-spirited Virginia gentleman, his concern for the welfare of his family grew into a sense of responsibility to serve the good of the community regardless of personal consequences, and his need for recognition and prestige became a will to merit the love and regard of his fellow citizens.

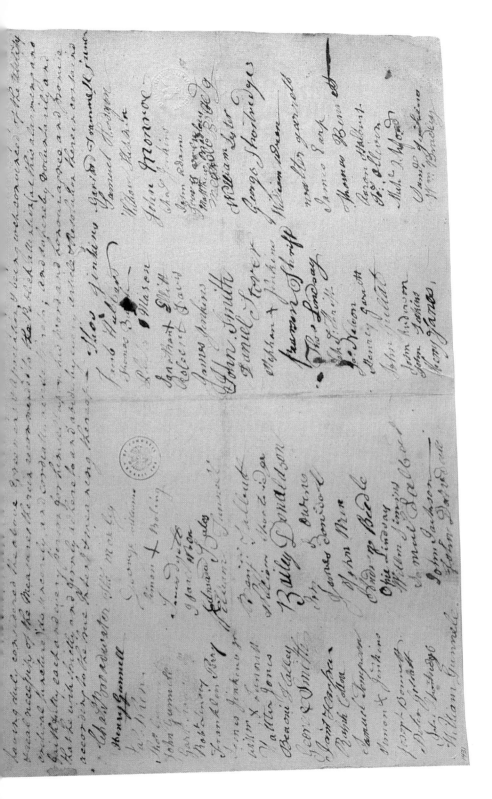

Washington arrived at his decision to support American independence in slow, sporadic steps over a period of years. As a planter marketing his crops in England, he felt the sting of restrictive trade acts passed by the British Parliament. As a Burgess he considered with his peers the merits of political appeal and retaliation. As a former officer he faced the increasing probability of military action.

Figure 112

Broadside of the Non-Importation Association, June 22, 1770, a response to growing interest in boycotting British goods and trade. Washington, a member of the committee which wrote the association, circulated copies of the broadside in Fairfax County for signatures.
Lent by the Library of Congress.

The exhibition also includes:

Letter from a Farmer in Pennsylvania to the Inhabitants of the British Colonies, by John Dickinson, 1768. George Washington bought a copy of this pamphlet while in Williamsburg in May 1769. *National Museum of American History.*

Letter with invoices from George Washington to Robert Cary and Company, July 25, 1769. Washington instructed his agent that *if there are any articles contained in either of the respective invoices ... which are Taxed by Act of Parliament for the Purpose of Raising a Revenue in America, it is my express desire and request that they may not be sent.*
Lent by the Library of Congress.

Letter from the Fairfax Independent Company of Volunteers to George Washington, October 19, 1774, requesting him to buy colors, drums, fifes, and halberts. The company had been formed September 21, 1774, in response to continuing *deprication of American freedom* by the British.
Lent by the Library of Congress.

THE COMMAND: "IT HAS BEEN A KIND OF DESTINY THAT HAS THROWN ME UPON THIS SERVICE"

By 1775, when Washington arrived in Philadelphia as one of the delegates to the Second Continental Congress, he had methodically given "the subject the fairest consideration." The attitude resulting from these deliberations was manifest in his choosing to present himself at the civilian Congress, which was meeting to consider action against the British, in military uniform.

The delegates were acutely aware of the need for a military leader who would elicit respect and a sense of unity throughout the colonies. Washington had already established a reputation for military leadership that crossed colonial borders. Combined with his personal dignity and self-control, his social confidence, and his political experience, his appearance in uniform made a powerful impression upon the delegates. It was only natural, then, that when the Congress decided to establish an American Continental Army, Washington—"the gentleman from Virginia"—was unanimously elected to the command.

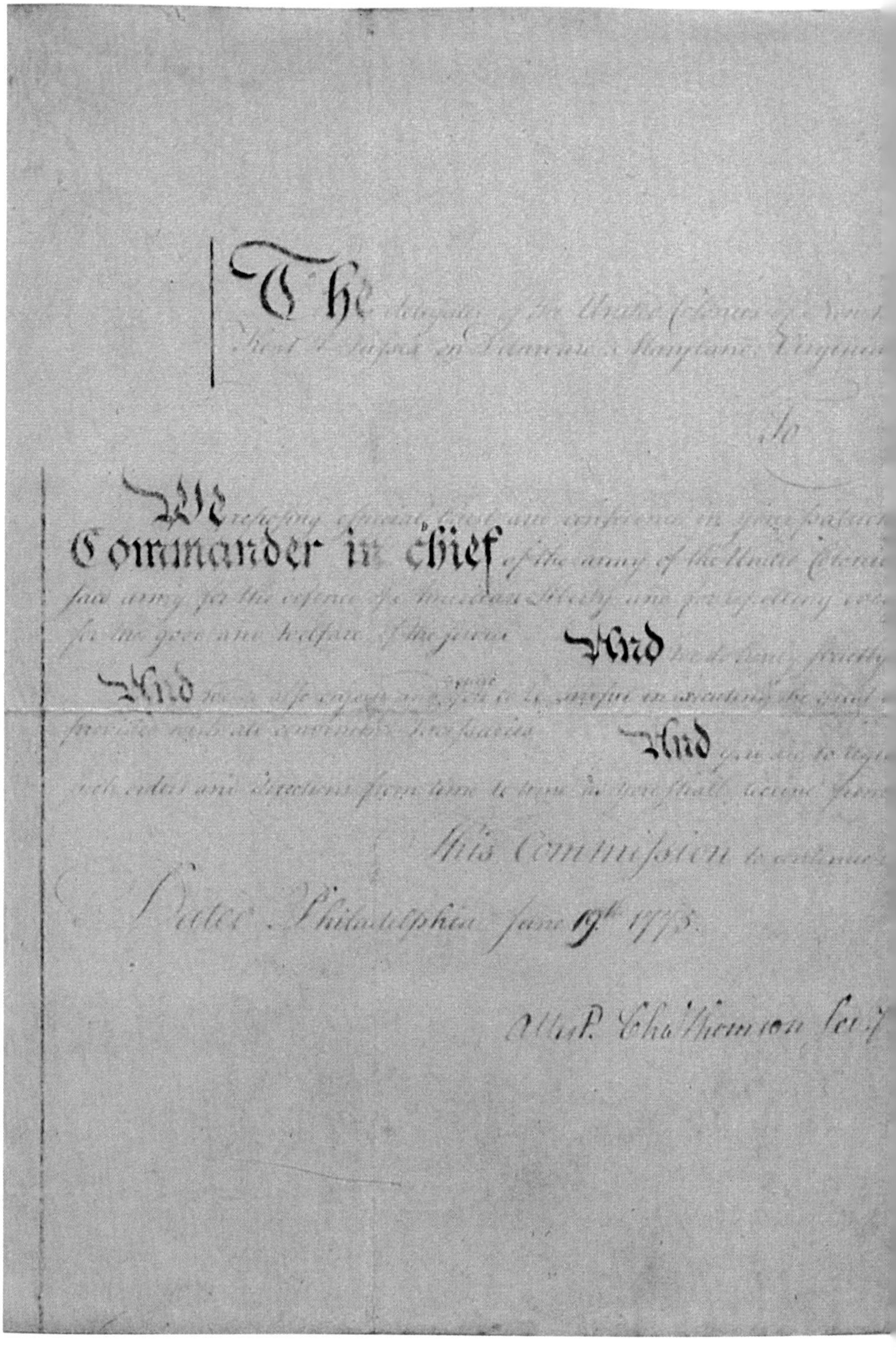
The

Commander in chief

And

And

And

This Commission

Dated Philadelphia June 19th 1775

Figure 113
George Washington's Commission as General and Commander in Chief of the Army of the United Colonies, June 19, 1775, signed by John Hancock, President of the Continental Congress.
Lent by the Library of Congress.

In Congress

[The Massachusetts Bay, Rhode Island, Connecticut, New York, New Jersey, Pennsylvania ... ... Carolina & South Carolina]

George Washington Esquire

DO by these presents constitute and appoint you to be General and ...

... of all the forces raised or to be raised by them and of all others who shall voluntarily offer their service ...

... And you are hereby vested with the power and authority to act ...

... require all officers and soldiers under your command to be obedient ...

... by causing strict discipline and order to be observed ...

... until altered by this or a future Congress.

By order of the Congress

John Hancock President

THE COMMANDER IN CHIEF:
"MY REPUTATION"

After George Washington accepted the command of the Revolutionary Army in 1775, he became continually concerned about his personal reputation and anxious to appear well in the eyes of others.

In 1776, after a dreadful showing at the skirmish that became known as the Battle of Harlem Heights, Washington wrote Lund Washington admitting his despair—a despair ultimately entwined with concern for his personal dignity and reputation as well as his anxiety about the fate of the army and the revolutionary cause. He wrote, "I see the impossibility of serving with reputation, or doing any essential service to the cause by continuing in command, and yet I am told that if I quit the command inevitable ruin will follow from the distraction that will ensue. I tell you that I never was in such an unhappy, divided state since I was born."

Despite Washington's continued fear for his "reputation" and the rarity of his out-and-out victories during the Revolutionary War, he won renown and reputation as a successful military leader. Perhaps Washington's greatest feat of command was the very fact he was able to sustain his army under prevailing conditions.

Washington kept together an ever-changing conglomeration of untrained people of every description. He kept the assemblage functioning by establishing networks of communication, imposing order and regularity, and demanding recognition of social and military proprieties. He kept his men alive, personally supervising such mundane matters as how food was prepared. In response to the superior military force of the enemy, he kept his small fighting force too mobile, too quick, too well positioned to be trapped and crushed completely.

By the time the war ended in 1783, George Washington had served eight and a half years as Commander in Chief. He had survived the long conflict with his reputation not only intact but greatly enhanced. He wrote, "Nothing now remains but for the actors of this mighty scene to preserve a perfect, unvarying constancy of character through the very last act, to close the drama with applause, and to retire from the military theater with the same approbation of angels and men which have crowned all their former virtuous actions."

Figure 114
A Map of the States of New York and New Jersey . . .
Delineated for the use of His Excely Genl Washington,
by Robt. Erskine, F.R.S. 1777.
Lent by The Pierpont Morgan Library.

The exhibition also includes:

The Theatre of War in North America . . . By an
American, a map printed in London for Robert
Sayer and John Bennett, November 20, 1776.
National Museum of American History.

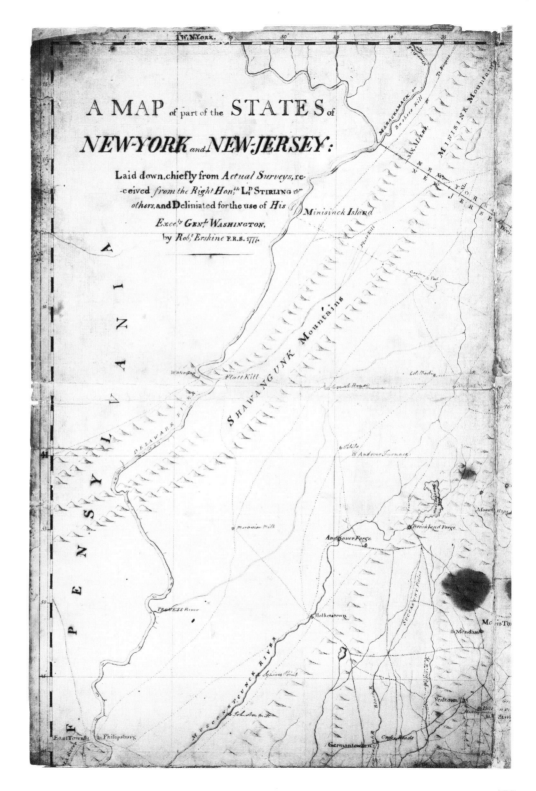

A MAP of part of the STATES of

NEW-YORK and NEW-JERSEY:

Laid down, chiefly from *Actual Surveys*, received *from the Right Hon.ble L.d Stirling &*
others, and Deliniated for the use of His
Exce.ly Gen.l Washington,
by Rob.t Erskine F.R.S. 1777.

THE ACCOUTREMENTS OF A GENERAL: "A RIBBON TO DISTINGUISH MYSELF"

As a gentleman, Washington had learned the necessity of establishing oneself in a "uniformly handsome and genteel manner" and the importance of distinguishing among social classes. As an aide to General Braddock, he had noted the style in which a British general campaigned and become convinced of the utility of maintaining proper distinctions of rank. As a Colonel of the Virginia Regiment he had concluded that the "character and appearance" of officers is important because "the person commanded yields but reluctant obedience to those he conceives are undeservedly made his superiors."

These lessons from experience, as well as the need to make the ragtag Continental Army appear to the enemy to be a legitimate professional military organization, prompted Washington to demand the deference due a commanding general, present himself carefully "in the Character of a Gentleman," and equip himself with the proper accoutrements.

Figure 115
Silver camp cup engraved with George Washington's crest. Washington purchased two dozen cups from William Hollingshead, a silversmith in Philadelphia, in March 1776 for £11.7.1.
National Museum of American History.

The exhibition also includes:

Camp stool with folding walnut frame, original cover replaced by leather. Plunket Fleeson billed Washington for *18 Wallnut camp Stools, moreen, brass nails, girth tack & bottoming* at a cost of £13.10.
National Museum of American History.

Figure 116
Tent and carrying bag. Washington ordered
headquarters tents from Plunket Fleeson of
Philadelphia in May, 1776.
National Museum of American History.

Believing that "nothing adds more to the Appearance of a man, than dress," Washington took special care to outfit himself in a fashion suitable to his rank.

Figure 117
Field glass and case used by Washington. Such *spy-glasses . . . constituted part of my equipage during the late war.*
From the Lewis Collection,
National Museum of American History.

Figure 118
Uniform worn by General George Washington.
Family tradition identifies it as the one he wore
when he resigned his commission at Annapolis in
1783.
National Museum of American History.

The exhibition also includes:

George Washington at Princeton, 1779, by Charles
Willson Peale.
Oil on canvas, 93″ × 58½″.
Lent by the Mount Vernon Ladies' Association.

One of a pair of silver spurs *presented to Lieut.
Thomas by Genl. Washington's taking them from his
own Boots, while giving his orders to Lieut. Lamb at
Valley Forge in Jany. 1778, to proceed to Boston for
Supplies for the Army.* This history was engraved on
the spur at a later date.
Lent by the Mount Vernon Ladies' Association.

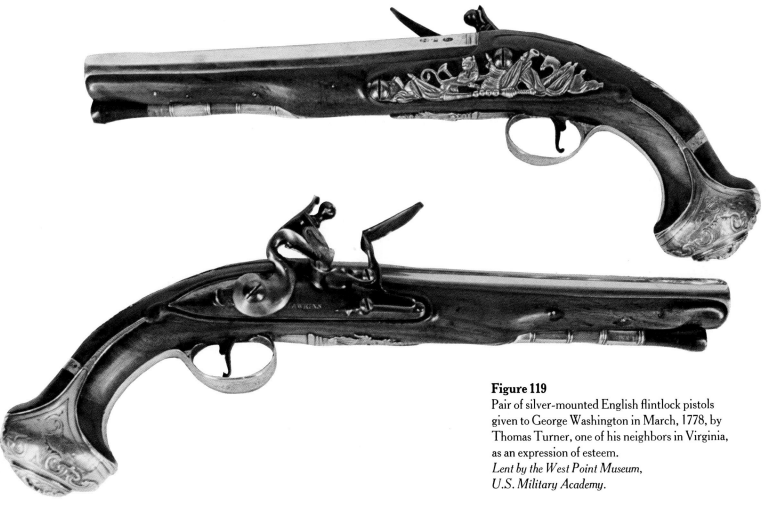

Figure 119
Pair of silver-mounted English flintlock pistols
given to George Washington in March, 1778, by
Thomas Turner, one of his neighbors in Virginia,
as an expression of esteem.
*Lent by the West Point Museum,
U.S. Military Academy.*

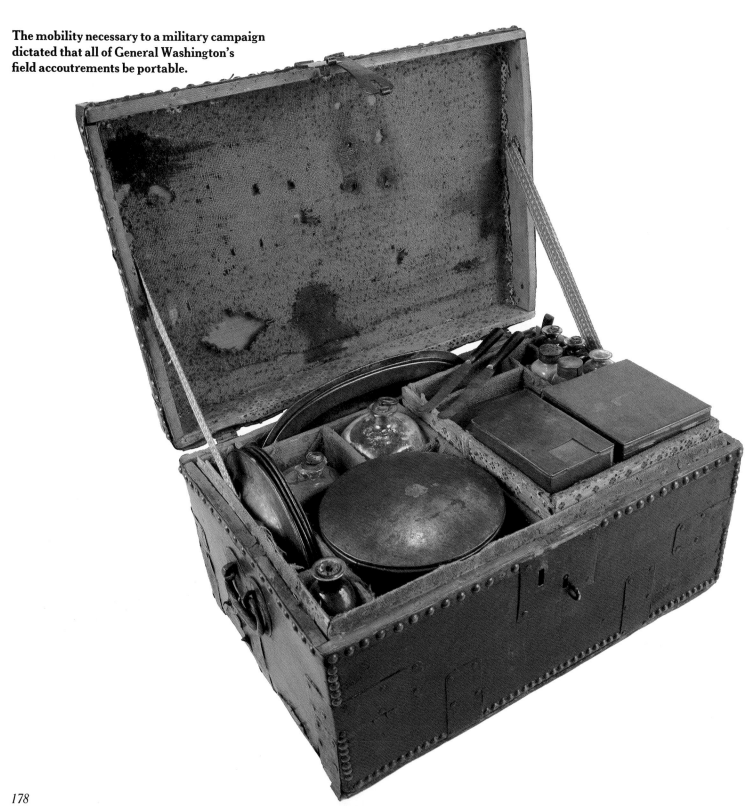

The mobility necessary to a military campaign dictated that all of General Washington's field accoutrements be portable.

Figure 120

George Washington's mess chest, equipped with four tin pots with detachable wooden handles, five tin plates, three tin platters, two tin boxes, two knives, three forks, a gridiron with collapsible legs, a tinder box, eight glass bottles with cork stoppers, two glass bottles with pewter tops for salt and pepper, and a woolen sack with six compartments. *National Museum of American History.*

The exhibition also includes:

Field bed used by General George Washington during the American Revolution, given to him by Continental Army Colonel Peter Gansevoort Jr. of New York.
Lent by the Edison Institute.

"Rose" blanket of the type commonly used in the field during the Revolutionary War, owned by General Washington. The term "rose" comes from the roses embroidered in the four corners of the blanket.
From the Peter Collection.
National Museum of American History.

George Washington's shaving case with mirror.
From the Lewis Collection,
National Museum of American History.

Figure 121

Battle sword carried by George Washington during the War. Washington left his swords to his nephews with *an injunction not to unsheath them for the purpose of shedding blood, except it be for self defence, or in defence of their Country and its rights; and in the latter case, to keep them unsheathed, and prefer falling with them in their hands to the relinquishment thereof.*
National Museum of American History.

THE ARMY: "TREAT THEM WITH AFFIBILITY & COURTESIE"

By the force of his personality, Washington held the Revolutionary Army together in the face of overwhelming odds, limited enlistments, and shortages of food, clothing, and even arms and ammunition. Even though he maintained sharp distinctions among himself, his officers, and his men, he was also careful to create a sense of unity with him among all ranks. The vast majority of Washington's men had only respect and affection for their leader. Abigail Adams seems to have best caught the essence of the General when she wrote, soon after meeting him when he arrived in Boston to take command, that he "has a dignity that forbids familiarity, mixed with an easy affibility that creates love and reverence."

THE OFFICERS

Washington recognized that his officers were "men of Quality," socially "equal or not much inferior" to himself, and he treated them with "great politeness." Yet, although Washington could on occasion "throw off the hero" and "take up the chatty agreeable companion," exchanging pleasantries and ribald humor, he took pains to preserve the dignity of his position. "Be easy and condescending in your disposition to your officers," he wrote in 1775, "but not too familiar, lest you subject yourself to a want of that respect which is necessary to support a proper command."

Figure 122
Washington and His Generals at Yorktown,
by Charles Willson Peale, c.1781.
Oil on canvas, $21\frac{3}{8}'' \times 29\frac{9}{16}''$.
Lent by the Maryland Historical Society; gift of Robert Gilmor Jr.

The exhibition also includes:

The Yankey's return from Camp. Broadside with an early version of Yankee Doodle:
And there was captain Washington,
And gentlefolks about him,
They say he's grown so tarnal proud,
He will not ride without 'em.
Eighteenth-century custom dictated that the commanding general always be surrounded by his staff. The custom was not always appreciated by the men.
Lent by the American Antiquarian Society.

Manoeuvers, by William Young, London, 1771. Washington advised his officers to "devote the vacant moments they may have to the study of Military authors."
Lent by the Boston Athenaeum.

Company roll and muster of Washington's Guards, 1782. In 1776, Washington had formed this unit of *men . . . neat and spruce* expressly to safeguard his person, papers, and personal effects.
National Museum of American History.

Letter from George Washington to the President of the Continental Congress, February 11, 1777. Washington welcomed the assistance of the professional soldiers provided through the alliance with France but deplored those that were *entirely useless as officers, from their ignorance of the English Language.*
Lent by the National Archives and Records Service.

THE TROOPS

Washington regarded many of his men, particularly those in the militia, as "exceeding dirty and nasty people," yet he treated them as individuals who had rights as well as duties. As a gentleman he had learned to treat people of "low Degree . . . with affibility & Courtesie, without Arrogancy." As a Virginia Colonel, he had learned that combining benevolence with "the strictest discipline" and "the strictest justice" could win him the confidence and admiration of his men. And as a General, he asked nothing of his men that he was not willing to do himself; while in the field he shared with them the physical hardships and shortages that plagued his army.

Figure 123
Battle of Princeton, by William Mercer.
Oil on canvas, $25\frac{1}{4}'' \times 40\frac{1}{2}''$.
A contemporary painting of Washington leading his men.
Lent by the Historical Society of Pennsylvania.

The exhibition also includes:

Regulations For the Order and Discipline of the Troops of the United States, by Friedrich Wilhelm A.H.F. von Steuben. When Baron von Steuben arrived at Valley Forge in February 1778, he found the army in winter quarters, threadbare and *with regard to military discipline . . . no such thing existed.* Appalled, the professional soldier personally wrote a drill book and started to train the troops.
Lent by the Library of Congress.

Orderly book kept at General Washington's headquarters at Valley Forge, May 18 to June 11, 1778.
Lent by the Boston Athenaeum.

THE CONGRESS: "UNDER WHOSE ORDERS I HAVE SO LONG ACTED"

As Commander in Chief, Washington was the ultimate authority in the Continental Army, a fact he made plain to his officers and men. He was careful to acknowledge, however, that he had assumed command in "Congress's name" and was acting only as an agent to a higher, civilian authority. Washington understood the importance of recognizing the limits of power and deferring to "they that are in Dignity or in office." And as General, he recognized that he and his Army were subservient to the Congress.

During the course of the war, Washington was constantly in communication with the delegates, advising them of events and soliciting instructions. Although at times he was annoyed by their inactivity and resentful of their demands, he had learned long before to "strive not with your Superiors in argument." His deference to civilian authority was to set the pattern for future American armies.

Figure 124
Portable writing case with compartments for paper, pens, pencils, and sealing wax used by George Washington during the War.
From the Lewis Collection,
National Museum of American History.

The exhibition also includes:

Letter from George Washington to the President of Congress, December 16, 1776, in which he implores Congress to increase the size of the Army and provide adequate clothing for the troops on hand.
Lent by the National Archives and Records Service.

Letter from George Washington to the President of Congress, August 31, 1779, in which he rescinds an order in response to directions from the Congress.
Lent by the National Archives and Records Service.

Letter from George Washington to the President of Congress, October 19, 1781, announcing the *Reduction of the British Army under the Command of Lord Cornwallis* at Yorktown, Virginia.
Lent by the National Archives and Records Service.

Letter from George Washington to the President of Congress, December 20, 1783, requesting an appointment with the Congress in order to *resign the Commission I have the honor of holding in their Service.*
Lent by the National Archives and Records Service.

Figure 125
Medal commemorating the Battle of Boston, 20th century striking. In 1775 the Congress voted to award Washington a gold medal struck in Paris by the famous French engraver Du Vivier.
National Museum of American History.

THE SOCIETY OF THE CINCINNATI: "FRATERNAL BOND AMONG THE HEROES"

With the end of the War in 1783, the officers of the Continental Army formalized the bond of their common experience by forming an organization which they called the Society of the Cincinnati.

One of the founding provisions of the Society made membership hereditary to descendants of the original members. The rule was greeted with outrage by those who feared the establishment of a peerage in the new republic. Even Europeans joined in the outcry against this perceived threat to the ideals for which the Revolution had been fought. The controversy put Washington, who had been elected President General of the Society, in an uncomfortable position. He was embarrassed by the reaction to the hereditary rule and by calls that he resign. Washington did not involve himself in the public debate, but he privately insisted that the rule be dropped. Faced with his displeasure and at his insistence, the Society dropped the hereditary aspect of membership in 1784, only to reinstate it after his death.

Washington's personal pride in the organization and his position in it is reflected in an order he sent to France for membership badges for himself and his military aides. In 1786 he also purchased a service of Chinese export porcelain decorated with the insignia of the Society.

Figure 126
President General's *eagle*, the Society of the Cincinnati. This badge, set with diamonds, was a gift to Washington from officers of the French Navy in 1784.
Lent by The Society of the Cincinnati.

Figure 127

Pamphlets relating to the Society of the Cincinnati controversy. *Considerations on the Society or Order of the Cincinnati*, a pamphlet by *Cassius* (the pseudonym of Aedanus Burke) published in America in 1783, was the first attack leveled against the Society. The Society was defended against its detractors in *Observations on a Late Pamphlet . . . by an Obscure Individual*, published in Philadelphia in 1783. *Considerations sur L'Ordre de Cincinnatus*, published in London in 1784, was a French translation of Burke's original pamphlet by the Comte de Mirabeau distributed to embarrass Lafayette and other French officers who wore the Society's badge at the French court. De Mirabeau published an edition in English as *Considerations on the Order of the Cincinnatus* in London in 1785 for circulation to English audiences. The binding was applied to the pamphlets shown at a later date.
Lent by The Society of the Cincinnati.

The exhibition also includes:

Certificate of Membership in the Society of the Cincinnati granted to William Clark, signed by George Washington at Mount Vernon, March 1, 1787.
National Museum of American History.

Chinese export porcelain bowl with insignia of the Society of the Cincinnati, from the service purchased by Washington in 1786.
National Museum of American History.

. . . If I had been permitted to indulge my first and fondest wish, I should have remained in a private station. Although neither the present age or Posterity may possibly give me full credit for the feelings which I have experienced on the subject; yet I have a consciousness that nothing short of an absolute conviction of duty could ever have brought me upon the scenes of public life again.

> —George Washington to
> Catherine Macaulay Graham
> January 9, 1790

THE INTERIM: "A GREATER DRAMA"

A greater drama is now being acted on this theatre than has heretofore been brought on the American stage, or any other in the world. We exhibit at present the novel and astounding spectacle of a whole people deliberating calmly on what forms of government will be most conducive to their happiness.

> —George Washington to
> Sir Edward Newenham
> August 29, 1788

WE the People of the States of New-Hampshire, Massachusetts, Rhode-Island and Providence Plantations, Connecticut, New-York, New-Jersey, Pennsylvania, Delaware, Maryland, Virginia, North-Carolina, South-Carolina, and Georgia, do ordain, declare and establish the following Constitution for the Government of Ourselves and our Posterity.

ARTICLE I.

The stile of this Government shall be, " The United States of America."

II.

The Government shall consist of supreme legislative, executive and judicial powers.

III.

The legislative power shall be vested in a Congress, to consist of two separate and distinct bodies of men, a House of Representatives, and a Senate; ~~each of which shall, in all cases, have a negative on the other. The Legislature shall meet on the first Monday in December in every year.~~

IV.

Sect. 1. The Members of the House of Representatives shall be chosen every second year, by the people of the several States comprehended within this Union. The qualifications of the electors shall be the same, from time to time, as those of the electors in the several States, of the most numerous branch of their own legislatures.

Sect. 2. Every Member of the House of Representatives shall be of the age of twenty-five years at least; shall have been a citizen of the United States for at least [...] years before his election; and shall be, at the time of his election, [...] of the State in which he shall be chosen.

Sect. 3. The House of Representatives shall, at its first formation, and until the number of citizens and inhabitants shall be taken in the manner herein after described, consist of sixty-five Members, of whom three shall be chosen in New-Hampshire, eight in Massachusetts, one in Rhode-Island and Providence Plantations, five in Connecticut, six in New-York, four in New-Jersey, eight in Pennsylvania, one in Delaware, six in Maryland, ten in Virginia, five in North-Carolina, five in South-Carolina, and three in Georgia.

Sect. 4. As the proportions of numbers in the different States will alter from time to time; as some of the States may hereafter be divided; as others may be enlarged by addition of territory; as two or more States may be united; as new States will be erected within the limits of the United States, the Legislature shall, in each of these cases, regulate the number of representatives by the number of inhabitants, according to the [...] rate of one for every forty thousand. Provided that every State shall have at least one representative.

Sect. 5. All bills for raising or appropriating money, and for fixing the salaries of the officers of government, shall originate in the House of Representatives, and shall not be altered or amended by the Senate. No money shall be drawn from the public Treasury, but in pursuance of appropriations that shall originate in the House of Representatives.

Sect. 6. The House of Representatives shall have the sole power of impeachment. It shall choose its Speaker and other officers.

Sect. 7. Vacancies in the House of Representatives shall be supplied by writs of election from the executive authority of the State, in the representation from which they shall happen.

V.

188

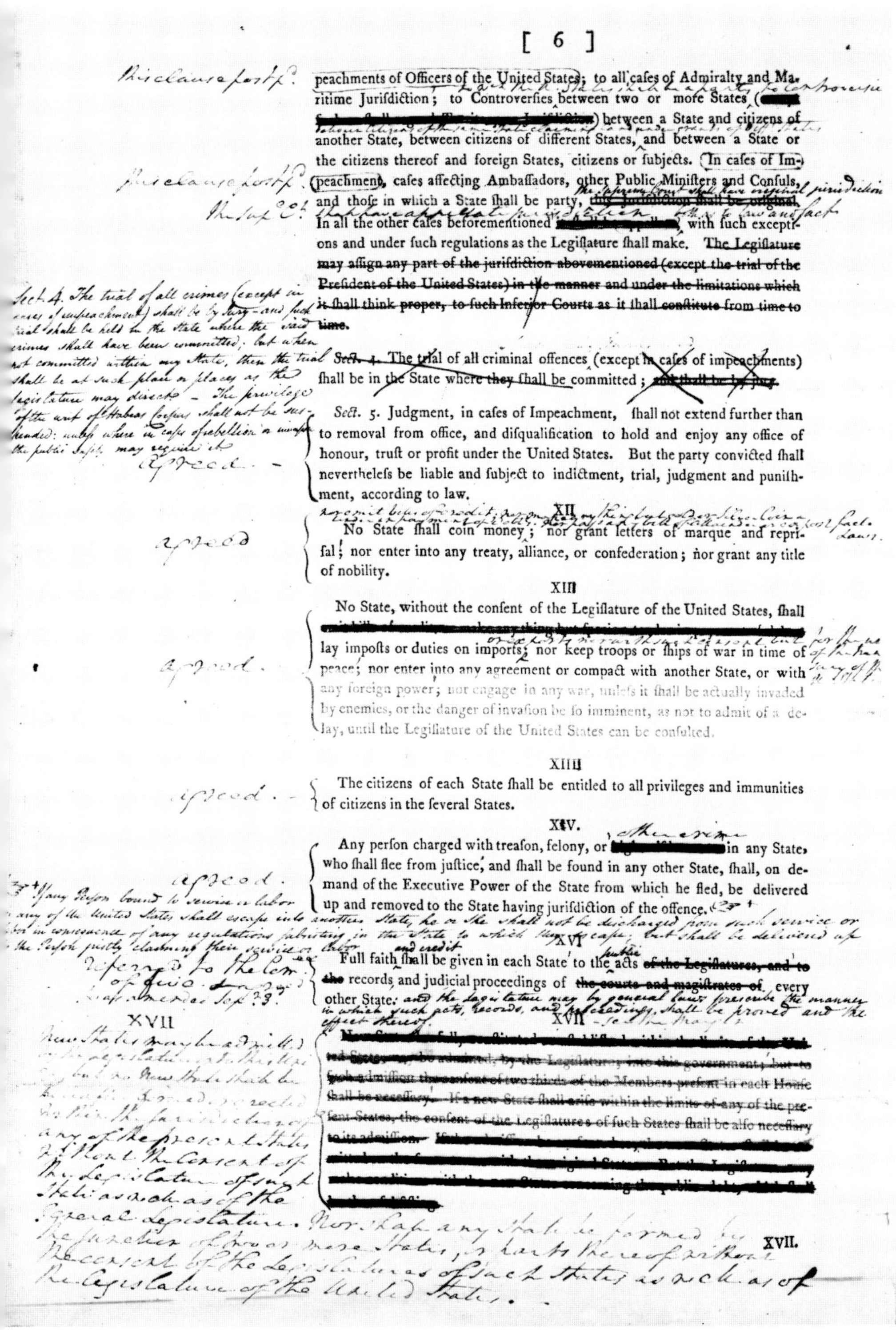

peachments of Officers of the United States; to all cases of Admiralty and Maritime Jurisdiction; to Controversies between two or more States; between a State and citizens of another State, between citizens of different States, and between a State or the citizens thereof and foreign States, citizens or subjects. In cases of Impeachment, cases affecting Ambassadors, other Public Ministers and Consuls, and those in which a State shall be party, In all the other cases beforementioned with such exceptions and under such regulations as the Legislature shall make. The Legislature may assign any part of the jurisdiction abovementioned (except the trial of the President of the United States) in the manner and under the limitations which it shall think proper, to such Inferior Courts as it shall constitute from time to time.

Sect. 4. The trial of all criminal offences (except in cases of impeachments) shall be in the State where they shall be committed; and shall be by jury.

Sect. 5. Judgment, in cases of Impeachment, shall not extend further than to removal from office, and disqualification to hold and enjoy any office of honour, trust or profit under the United States. But the party convicted shall nevertheless be liable and subject to indictment, trial, judgment and punishment, according to law.

XII

No State shall coin money; nor grant letters of marque and reprisal; nor enter into any treaty, alliance, or confederation; nor grant any title of nobility.

XIII

No State, without the consent of the Legislature of the United States, shall lay imposts or duties on imports; nor keep troops or ships of war in time of peace; nor enter into any agreement or compact with another State, or with any foreign power; nor engage in any war, unless it shall be actually invaded by enemies, or the danger of invasion be so imminent, as not to admit of a delay, until the Legislature of the United States can be consulted.

XIIII

The citizens of each State shall be entitled to all privileges and immunities of citizens in the several States.

XIV

Any person charged with treason, felony, or in any State, who shall flee from justice, and shall be found in any other State, shall, on demand of the Executive Power of the State from which he fled, be delivered up and removed to the State having jurisdiction of the offence.

XVI

Full faith shall be given in each State to the acts of the Legislatures, and to the records and judicial proceedings of the courts and magistrates of every other State.

XVII

For six years after resigning his command of the Continental Army, George Washington "tread the private walks of life with heartfelt satisfaction," concerning himself once again with the business and pleasures of a gentleman's life and enjoying "freedom from public cares."

Yet as the years progressed, Washington became aware that he could not ignore the problems that were cropping up in the government under the Articles of Confederation. He feared that the "half-starved, limping Government, that appears always to be moving upon crutches & tottering at every step" was going to collapse. He was convinced that the government needed to be "braced and held with a steady hand." Thus, when supporters of a stronger government called a Convention to revise the federal constitution, Washington reluctantly agreed to participate.

Washington joined delegates from each state in Philadelphia in May of 1787. Unanimously elected President of the Convention, he lent to the proceedings an air of power and legitimacy. Although Washington took great pains not to involve himself in any of the formal debates, he followed them closely; his very presence (and perhaps his unrecorded exertions) influenced the proceedings. "Be assured," wrote James Madison of Washington's role, "his influence carried the government."

Figure 128
Copy of the final draft of the United States Constitution on which Washington made notes while he presided at the Convention.
Lent by the National Archives and Records Service.

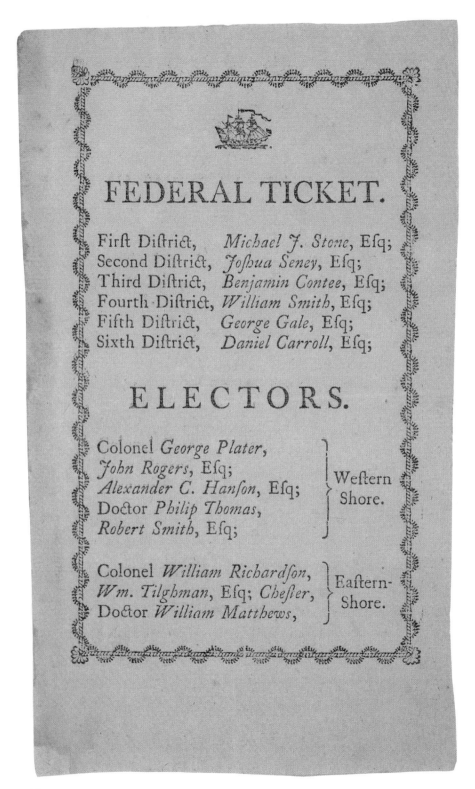

Figure 129
Federal electoral ticket broadside for the State of Maryland, 1789.
National Museum of American History.

The exhibition also includes:

Letter to George Washington from John Langdon, President pro tempore of the Senate, April 6, 1789, notifying Washington of his election to the Presidency.
Lent by the Library of Congress.

THE RETURN: "PAINFUL SENSATIONS"

About ten o'clock I bade adieu to Mount Vernon, to private life, and to domestic felicity, and with a mind oppressed with more anxious and painful sensations than I have words to express, set out for New York . . . with the best disposition to render service to my country in obedience to its call, but with less hope of answering its expectations.

—George Washington in his *Diary*
April 16, 1789

Two years after the Federal Convention in Philadelphia, the new Constitution had been ratified, Washington had been nominated for the presidency, and a unanimous decision by the Electoral College had returned him to a role in the national theatre.

Washington did not want to return from the wings to center stage. From his previous experience he knew "too much of the vanity of human affairs to expect felicity from the splendid scenes of public life." He was wracked by the painful knowledge that the "loud acclamations of the people" could change to equally boisterous censure should his actions not correspond to their "sanguine expectations." His sole desire was to remain a farmer at Mount Vernon.

Nevertheless, Washington accepted the Presidency. His deeply ingrained sense of the obligations of a gentleman would not permit him to do otherwise. His belief in duty, his hunger for esteem, and his sense of leadership had overwhelmed his preference for comfortable privacy repeatedly during three decades of public service. So Washington embarked upon the Presidency, once again fulfilling his perceived obligations at the cost of "all expectations of private happiness in this world."

Figure 130
Commemorative clothing buttons worn by spectators at Washington's first inauguration. *National Museum of American History.*

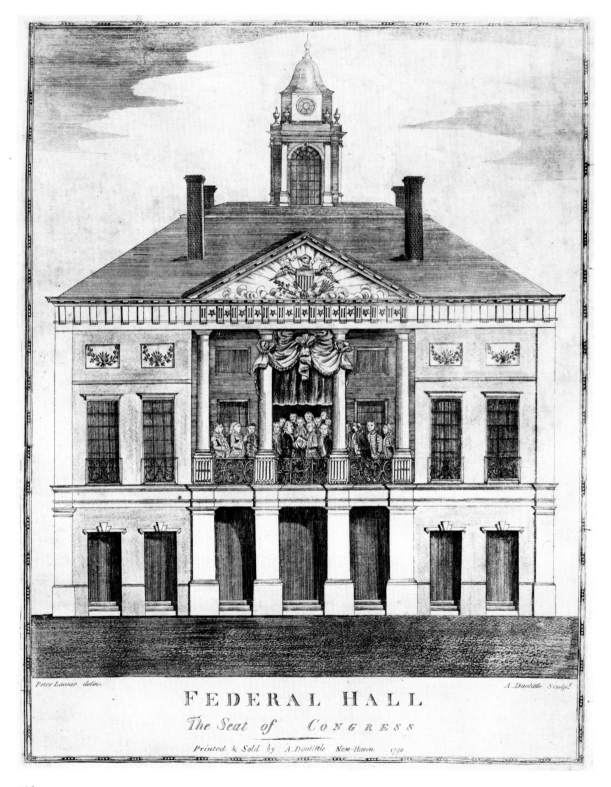

Peter Lacour delin.

A. Doolittle Sculp.

FEDERAL HALL

The Seat of CONGRESS

Printed & Sold by A. Doolittle New-Haven 1790

Figure 131
Federal Hall/the Seat of Congress, an engraving by Amos Doolittle depicting Washington's inauguration in New York City on April 29, 1789.
Lent by the Henry Francis du Pont Winterthur Museum.

Figure 132
Sheet music of *The New President's March* and *Washington's March*, sold at J. Paff's Music Store in New York City on the occasion of Washington's inauguration.
National Museum of American History.

THE PRESIDENT: "TO KEEP A PROPER STATE"

In our progress towards political happiness my station is new; and if I may use the expression, I walk on untrodden ground.

—George Washington to
Catherine Macaulay Graham
January 9, 1790

For the first time in his life Washington found himself in a role with no definite model after which to pattern his performance. There were no traditions, no precedents for the Presidency. His experience in other roles, however, led him to believe that the respect commanded by the new government would be determined in large part by the respect he could command for himself and his office. He therefore strived to create and maintain "a proper state," at once grand and simple, appropriate to the proper personification of the new government. He aimed always at a "republican stile."

In shaping the personal style of the president, he transferred the social proprieties and gentlemanly lifestyle of Mount Vernon to the Presidential Mansion. He surrounded himself with trappings "uniformly handsome and genteel" in order to give the newly established position the impression of elegance, dignity, stability.

Figure 133
Household furnishings from Mount Vernon. The Sheraton mahogany side chairs are listed in Washington's household account book as being purchased from Philadelphia cabinetmaker John Aiken in 1797. An arrangement of glassware from Mount Vernon is shown on the mahogany china table, c. 1770.
From the Lewis Collection,
National Museum of American History.

The exhibition also includes:

Hepplewhite mahogany arm chair. Two chairs of this design were purchased from Thomas Burling, a New York cabinet maker, for use in the Presidential Mansion in 1790.
From the Lewis Collection,
National Museum of American History.

The exhibition also includes:

Mirror with gilded frame, American, c.1790, which George Washington probably purchased for the Presidential Mansion in Philadelphia.
From the Lewis Collection,
National Museum of American History.

Silver-plated Argand lamps, wall bracket type, which Washington ordered from France through Gouvenor Morris in 1790.
From the Lewis Collection,
National Museum of American History.

Pieces of gold and white Sèvres porcelain from the service which George Washington purchased in 1790 from the Comte de Moustier, French Minister to the United States. This porcelain was used as the banquet service during Washington's presidency and later at Mount Vernon.
From the Lewis and Peter Collections,
National Museum of American History.

Bowl from a porcelain service given to Martha Washington on July 21, 1782, by the Comte de Custine-Sarreck, owner of the Niderviller factory in France and one of the French officers who fought with George Washington.
From the Lewis Collection,
National Museum of American History

Chinese export porcelain from *a Box of China for Lady Washington*, given her in 1796 by Andreas Everardus van Braam Houckgeest. The pieces were decorated with a chain motif to symbolize the strength of the Union, a snake to represent its perpetuity, and a motto upon a red ribbon scroll, *A Glory and a Defense of It*. Martha Washington's initials appear on the china against a sunburst of gold.
From the Lewis Collection,
National Museum of American History.

Tea chest covered with Chinese paper bearing polychrome decorations, owned by George Washington.
From the Lewis Collection,
National Museum of American History.

Inlaid rosewood and maple tray from the household furnishings at Mount Vernon.
National Museum of American History.

Painted copper decoration from the quarter-panel of the coach presented to Martha Washington as a gift from the people of Pennsylvania in 1777.
From the Patent Office Collection,
National Museum of American History.

Conch shell buttons. Always careful to appear elegant and fashionable in his personal attire, Washington purchased these buttons for his coat in Philadelphia during his presidency.
From the Peter Collection,
National Museum of American History.

Formal invitation to dinner. One of those used during the administration of George Washington to invite guests to dinner at the President's House.
National Museum of American History.

Message written by Washington's secretary to Abigail Adams, wife of Vice President John Adams, offering use of the President's box at a local theater. The theater had always been one of Washington's favorite recreations. As President, he enjoyed having a box and often shared it with his friends.
National Museum of American History.

Receipt for *Sundries for a President's Household*, December 28, 1795.
National Museum of American History.

Chippendale mahogany side chair used by the Washingtons in the Presidential Mansion in Philadelphia.
From Karl Richmond,
National Museum of American History.

Figure 134

Silver chest and silver owned by George Washington. The brassbound mahogany chest lined with green baize was used by George Washington to hold and transport large pieces of silver. According to family tradition, this chest was given him by his half-brother Lawrence. The candlestick is Sheffield plate. A cash memorandum for November 1783 lists the purchase of *Plated Candle Sticks @ 2½ Guins pr pair. Bread basket, large oval Waiter, Bottle Stands, pair Salts—blue glass* were all used by George Washington in the Presidential Mansion and are so listed under *Plate and Plated Ware* in the summary of "Household Furniture" made by Washington when he left Philadelphia in 1799. The silver-handle knives and forks, engraved with the Washington crest, were purchased from London in 1757.
From the Lewis Collection,
National Museum of American History.

Figure 135
Silver-plated Argand table lamp which Washington
possibly purchased in 1792 from Philadelphia
silversmith Joseph Anthony.
From the Lewis Collection,
National Museum of American History.

Figure 136
Glassware used by George and Martha Washington
at the Presidential Mansion and at Mount Vernon.
From the Lewis and Peter Collections,
National Museum of American History.

THE PRESIDENCY: "THE DIFFICULT AND DELICATE PART"

Few who are not philosophical spectators can realize the difficult and delicate part, which a man in my situation has to act.

—George Washington to
Catherine Macaulay Graham
January 9, 1790

There is scarcely any part of my conduct which may not hereafter be drawn into precedent.

—George Washington to
Catherine Macaulay Graham
January 9, 1790

In shaping the administrative style of the presidency, Washington struggled to create a role for the office that was dignified, decorous, and aloof from political squabbling. Thirty-eight years earlier he had carefully noted during his visit with Lawrence to Barbados that the Govenor declined "much familiarity" and was a "Gentleman of good Sense" who "gives no handl[e] for complaint." After eight years as Commander in Chief of the Continental Army he had learned the pragmatic benefits of what Abigail Adams had called "a dignity that forbids familiarity, mixed with an easy affibility that creates love and reverence," and he was firm in his opinion that the best leader did not subject himself "to a want of that respect which is necessary to support a proper command."

Washington was intensely aware that the style and substance of his behavior as President would create the basic pattern within which all his successors to that office would act. His concern with even minor details was based on a perception that "many things which appear of little importance in themselves and at the beginning may have general and durable consequences from their having been established at the commencement of a new general government."

Washington was correct in his assumption that his presidency would determine the future nature of the office. His orderly habits of mind made him an effective administrator and—by creating a cabinet of department secretaries directly responsible to the president and insisting on complete autonomy in selecting presidential advisors of varying political opinions—he established a strong and centralized presidential authority. By his responses to specific political and policy questions, Washington also established prerogatives and limits for the office in dealing with the Congress and the people of the nation.

The exhibition also includes:

Journal of William Maclay, Senator from
Pennsylvania and one of the President's most
outspoken critics, open to the entry of August 27,
1789. Maclay recounts Washington's visit to the
Senate for advice and consent on the Indian Peace
Treaty. When the Senate postponed the discussion,
the President withdrew politely, but he never again
permitted the Senate to participate in the
negotiations for a treaty, restricting their role to
that of approving negotiations carried out by the
executive branch.
*Reproductions from the Collections of the Library
of Congress.*

Broadside issued by General Henry Lee
announcing the government's intention to quell the
Whiskey Rebellion by military force, 1794.
Washington had sent Lee to Western Pennsylvania
after local farmers challenged the right of the
Federal government to levy an excise tax on
whiskey.
Lent by the Library of Congress.

Figure 137
Silver peace medal given to "Red Jacket," Grand
Sachem of the Iroquois Indians, in 1792. The medal
depicts President George Washington, as the
symbol of the new nation, exchanging a gesture of
peace with an Indian.
Lent by the Buffalo and Erie County Historical Society.

*There is scarcely an action, the motive of which
may not be subject to a double interpretation.*
—George Washington to
Catherine Macaulay Graham
January 9, 1790

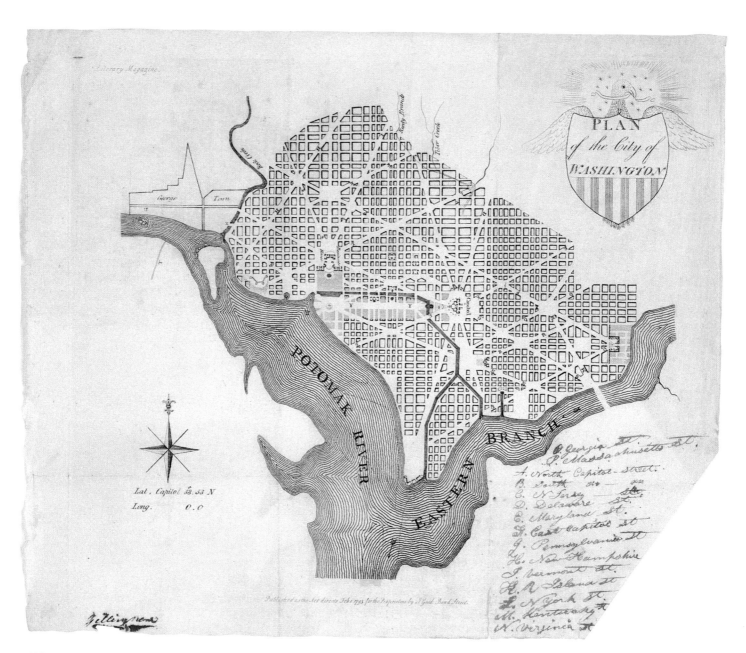

"I think I see a path, as clear and direct as a ray of light, which if pursued will ensure permanent felicity to the Commonwealth," wrote Washington before he assumed office. It was clear to him that "nothing but harmony, honesty, industry and frugality are necessary to make us a great and happy people."

Washington felt that the new nation's chief objective should be to recover from the economic disruption of the War by re-establishing credit, stimulating agricultural production, and encouraging manufacturing. It was in accordance with these goals that he embraced controversial measures such as Alexander Hamilton's monetary proposals.

The pathway to felicity was not, however, to be as direct as Washington had supposed. When the economic policies he endorsed appeared to favor the businessmen of the north over southern agrarian interests, the administration was attacked as having hidden motives. And even as Washington tried to maintain an air of balanced dignity, members of his cabinet split into opposing factions. His Secretary of Treasury, Alexander Hamilton, and his Secretary of State, Thomas Jefferson, feuded openly and fervently.

A compromise won Jefferson's support of the economic policies in return for Hamilton's agreement to establish the nation's capital in the South. Washington, who had detached himself from the confrontation, became enthusiastically involved in the creation of the "Grand Columbian Federal City," which was to bear the name of Washington. The truce between Hamilton and Jefferson, however, was to be short-lived.

The exhibition also includes:

Letter to George Washington from Daniel Hinsdale, March 23, 1789, discussing fabric manufactured in Hartford, Connecticut.
Lent by the Library of Congress.

Drawing of the carriage George Washington ordered while President in 1792, by E. Pratt, London. Watercolor. In the first year of his Presidency Washington set out in his "state" coach on a month's tour of New England that gave him firsthand knowledge of New England's commerce and manufacturing. His realization that economic development would bring the nation power and prestige led him to support the economic proposals of Alexander Hamilton.
Lent by the Edison Institute.

T-Square used by President Washington during the ceremonial laying of the cornerstone of the Capitol in September, 1793. Washington's Masonic Lodge No. 22 of Alexandria, Virginia, had made the arrangements for the dedication.
Lent by Alexamdria-Washington Lodge No. 22, A.F. & A.M.

How unfortunate & how much is it to be regretted then, that whilst we are encompassed on all sides with avowed enemies & insidious friends, that internal dissensions should be harrowing & tearing our vitals.
—George Washington to Thomas Jefferson
August 23, 1792

Despite his utmost effort to establish the role of a dignified, impartial executive, Washington soon discovered that his pathway to "felicity to the Commonwealth" was fraught with "Quicksands & mires" and "many a painful step." Struggle as he might to remain aloof from political quarreling, Washington found he could not restrain the factions that were developing in his administration around its two arch rivals, Hamilton and Jefferson. At the end of his first term in office, Washington seriously considered retiring to save his reputation. Instead he succumbed once again to his sense of obligation to a people, and was unanimously re-elected to office in 1793.

The exhibition also includes:

Letter from Eliza Powel to George Washington, November 4, 1792. Mrs. Samuel Powel, friend and confidant of President Washington on matters social and political, wrote persuasively that if he resigned, it would be said that when his reputation was threatened he *would take no further risks* for the people.
Lent by the Mount Vernon Ladies' Association.

United States Senate Journal, Second Congress, Second Session. The entry for February 13, 1793, records George Washington's unanimous election to a second term as President of the United States.
Lent by the National Archives and Records Service through the courtesy of the United States Senate.

Washington continued his efforts to keep the Presidency "above politics," but factions in his own administration and in Congress had split into rival camps—the Federalists and the Republicans. In February of 1793 Washington himself was drawn into the fray when anti-Federalist newspapers began to attack him personally. When he eventually embraced the Jay Treaty with Great Britain and adopted a stance of neutrality toward the revolution in France (both of which were unpopular with Jeffersonian Republicans), he became irrevocably identified with the Hamiltonian Federalists and opened himself to vehement partisan attack.

Figure 139

The Times, A Political Portrait, political cartoon, 1797. Washington, flanked by Federal troops, is pictured steering the coach of state through presumably dangerous Francophile Republicans as Thomas Jefferson tries to interfere with the progress of the coach. Benjamin Franklin Bache, editor of the *Aurora*—a Republican newspaper critical of Washington and the Federalists—is being crushed, as a dog lifts its leg on his paper. *Reproduced from the Collections of The New-York Historical Society.*

The exhibition also includes:

National Gazette, March 2, 1793. This Republican newspaper, published by Philip Freneau, contains the first personal attack made against Washington. *Lent by the Library of Congress.*

Look on this Picture and on This, a pro-Federalist cartoon. The images of George Washington as the leader and symbol of the Federalists and Thomas Jefferson as leader of the Republicans continued to be evoked in subsequent campaigns and prompted cartoons such as this one, published in 1807. *Lent by the Charles W. McAlpin (Print) Collection; Art, Prints and Photographs Division; The New York Public Library; Astor, Lenox and Tilden Foundations.*

The Cannibals are landing

TIMES, & POLITICAL PORTRAIT.

Volunteers

Step de wheels of

de gouvernement

Triumph Government, perish all its enemies.—
Traitors be warned: justice though slow, is sure.

x

Presented to the New York
State Historical Society,
By Geo B. Reed, Montpelier
Vermont.

THE FAREWELL: "THE MOST ARDENT WISHES OF MY HEART"

After eight years in office, Washington insisted that he should be allowed to retire to Mount Vernon. The nation was prospering and growing in size, domestic manufactures and foreign trade were booming, and a treaty signed with Spain had secured the American right to navigate the Mississippi River. Washington felt that despite frustration and physical exhaustion he had played well the "difficult and delicate part." He had kept the pledge he made to Henry Knox before taking office that, "Integrity and firmness is all I can promise."

Before giving up public life, Washington wanted to justify his actions as President and perform one more service as leader of the new nation. He wrote a last message to his countrymen, which revealed his insight and understanding of the path that the country should take, notions which are still evoked today.

Figure 140
Brass double candlestick, English, c.1770. Washington preferred to use this particular desk lamp while writing at night; family tradition tells of him using it as he worked on his Farewell Address.
From the Lewis Collection,
National Museum of American History.

The exhibition also includes:

Washington's Farewell Address to the People of the United States, published for the Washington Benevolent Society, printed and sold by Denio & Phelps, Greenfield, 1812. The Address was widely published in a variety of forms.
National Museum of American History.

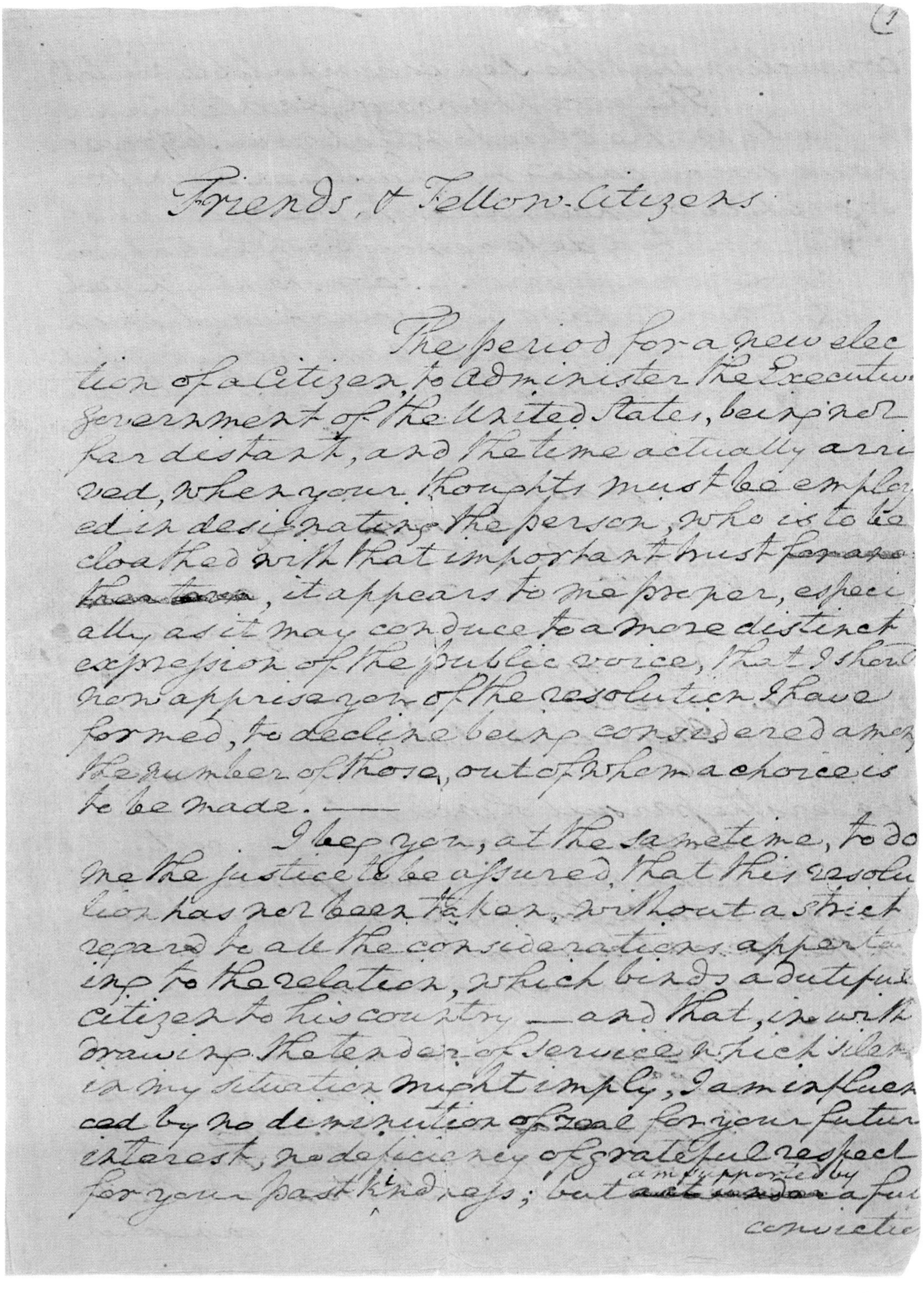

(1)

Friends, & Fellow-Citizens

The period for a new election of a Citizen, to administer the Executive Government of the United States, being not far distant, and the time actually arrived, when your thoughts must be employed in designating the person, who is to be cloathed with that important trust ~~for another term~~, it appears to me proper, especially as it may conduce to a more distinct expression of the public voice, that I should now apprise you of the resolution I have formed, to decline being considered among the number of those, out of whom a choice is to be made. —

I beg you, at the same time, to do me the justice to be assured, that this resolution has not been taken, without a strict regard to all the considerations appertaining to the relation, which binds a dutiful citizen to his country — and that, in withdrawing the tender of service which silence in my situation might imply, I am influenced by no diminution of zeal for your future interest, no deficiency of grateful respect for your past kindness; but ~~act under a~~ am supported by a full conviction

Figure 141
Manuscript of Washington's Farewell Address, *To the People of the United States*. Written for his *friends and fellow citizens*, the address was published in Claypoole's *American Daily Advertiser* on September 19, 1796. Washington had received help from James Madison on the first draft in 1792 and from Alexander Hamilton on the last, but the sentiments expressed were Washington's own.
Lent by the Rare Books and Manuscripts Division; The New York Public Library; Astor, Lenox and Tilden Foundations.

THE LASTING IMAGE:
"MR. STUARTS PAINTINGS"

George Washington, the Chief Executive, was immortalized in all his power and majesty by Gilbert Stuart in a portrait commissioned by William Bingham of Philadelphia. Bingham sent the original to his friend the Marquis of Lansdowne, an English aristocrat who had been a supporter of the American cause, but Stuart and others made copies of the portrait both for patrons at home and to send abroad to give credence to the new office and the new nation. A copy of the portrait hangs in the White House, where it has served as an inspiration of personal and administrative style to succeeding Presidents.

Figure 143
Portrait of George Washington, attributed to Gilbert Stuart.
Oil on canvas, 93″ × 59″.
Richard Warren Meade, U.S. Naval Agent in Cadiz, presented this portrait to the U.S. Embassy in Spain in 1818.
Lent by the United States Capitol through the Office of the Architect of the Capitol.

Figure 142
My fine crab-tree walking stick, with a gold head curiously wrought in the form of a liberty cap, which Benjamin Franklin bequeathed to *my friend, and the friend of mankind, General Washington.* Franklin wrote, *If it were a sceptre he has merited it and would become it.*
National Museum of American History.

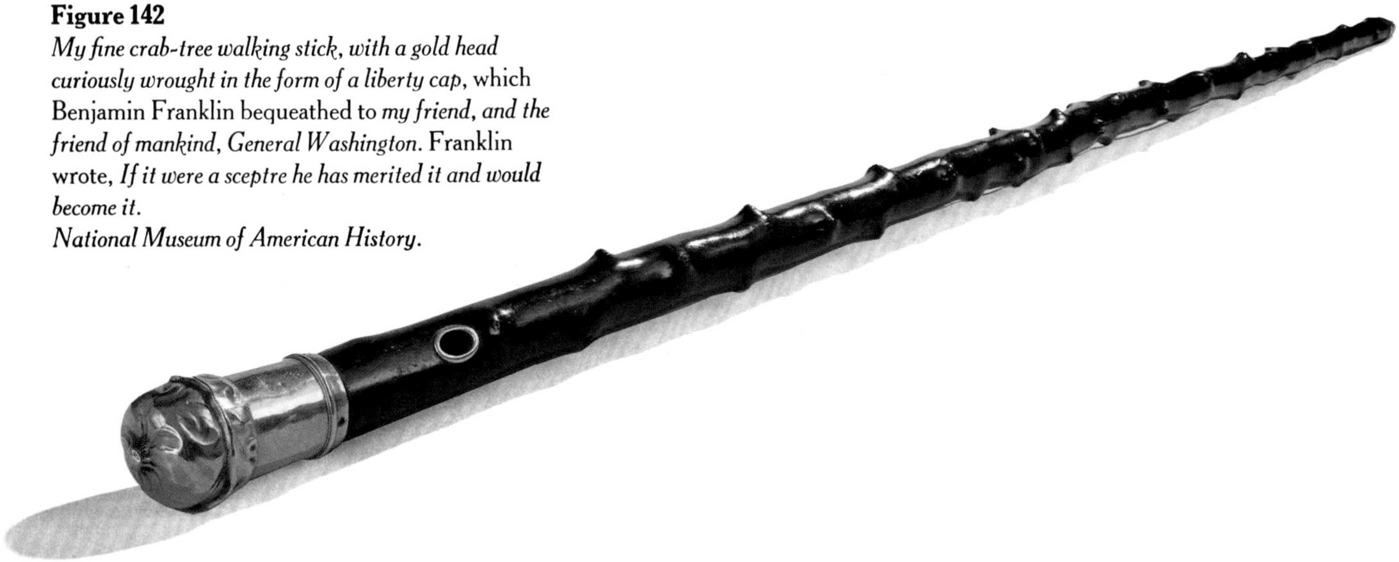

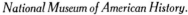

THE LAST ACT

*Indeed, the trouble and perplexities . . . added to the
weight of years which have passed over me, have worn
away my mind more than my body, and render ease and
retirement indispensably necessary to both during the
short time I have to stay here.*

—George Washington to John Jay
May 8, 1796

**George Washington was sixty-five when he left
the Presidency. As he rode to Mount Vernon
in a carriage with Martha, he carefully
avoided all public attentions, all parades or
escorts. He was tired of public life. He
likened himself to a weary traveller; he
wanted simply to go home.**

**All through his later life, Washington had
looked forward to retiring "under my own
vine and fig tree." After eight years
maneuvering through the "Quicksands &
mires" of the Presidency, he wanted to rest.
"I can truly say," he wrote, "I had rather be at
Mount Vernon with a friend or two about me
than to be attended at the Seat of Government
by the Officers and the Representatives of
every power in Europe."**

Figure 144
Portrait of George Washington,
by Rembrandt Peale, 1795.
Oil on canvas, $29\frac{3}{4}''\times 25\frac{1}{4}''$.
*Lent by the National Portrait Gallery;
gift of Andrew Mellon.*

THE RETIREMENT: "UNDER MY OWN VINE AND FIG TREE"

Washington was delighted once again to assume the role of farmer and hospitable neighbor. "To amuse myself in agricultural and rural pursuits," he wrote, "will constitute employment for the few years I have to remain on this terrestrial globe." He spent each day inspecting his land and crops on horseback, dressed in simple clothing and a broad-brimmed white hat and protected from the sun by an umbrella attached to his saddle. Every evening, he played host to the constant stream of visitors who came to pay their respects or, as Washington suspected, to satisfy their curiosity. A visitor to Mount Vernon recorded the dinner table conversation as "talk of many things: building improvements in the United States, bridges in particular, New England roads, mutual acquaintances, progress of public buildings in the Federal City, the weather, conditions of Crops, etc."

Figure 145
A View of Mount Vernon, by an American school artist, 1790 or later.
Oil on canvas, $37\frac{5}{8}'' \times 43\frac{3}{8}''$.
Lent by the National Gallery of Art; gift of Edgar William and Bernice Chrysler Garbisch.

VIEW OF MOUNT.VERNON THE SEAT OF GENERAL WASHINGTON.

Figure 146
Telescope made by "Cole, Fleet Street, London" and used at Mount Vernon for viewing boats on the Potomac.
From the Lewis Collection,
National Museum of American History.

Figure 147
Sketch of the Mount Vernon portico showing George Washington using his telescope, by Benjamin Henry Latrobe, 1796.
Lent from a private collection.

The exhibition also includes:

Print of
*Sketch of General Washington stolen at Mount
Vernon while he was looking to discover a distant
vessel on the Potomac . . .* by Benjamin Henry
Latrobe, 1796.
*Lent by the Maryland Historical Society,
Papers of Benjamin Henry Latrobe.*

Compass marked *Rittenhouse, Philadelphia,* used by
Washington at Mount Vernon. Washington was
known to have surveyed and resurveyed his own
land until the month before he died.
*From the Patent Office Collection,
National Museum of American History.*

Needle case made by Martha Washington
from scraps of dress fabric. Martha spent
many hours at sewing and embroidery both
for domestic purposes and as a
favorite recreation.
National Museum of American History.

Figure 148
Chess set and box with decorated cover, part
of the furnishings at Mount Vernon.
*From the Peter Collection,
National Museum of American History.*

Washington was physically "now past the grand climacteric." He was hard of hearing, he needed glasses for reading, he was bothered by pains. The teeth which he had so diligently cared for were gone entirely; the last one fell out in 1790, and his mouth was constantly irritated by ill-fitting dentures. He was still a man of imposing athletic stature, however, and he remained mentally astute.

The exhibition also includes:

Wing chair with footstool used in the Washingtons' bedroom at Mount Vernon.
From the Lewis Collection,
National Museum of American History.

Blue canton washbowl and water jug from Mount Vernon.
From the Lewis Collection,
National Museum of American History.

Water glass from Mount Vernon.
From the Lewis Collection,
National Museum of American History.

Blue canton water juglet from Mount Vernon.
From the Lewis Collection,
National Museum of American History.

Eyeglasses and case owned by George Washington.
Lent by the Mount Vernon Ladies' Association.

Brass Argand lamp from Mount Vernon.
From the Peter Collection,
National Museum of American History.

Lamp mat knitted by Martha Washington.
From the Lewis Collection,
National Museum of American History.

Figure 149
Cabinet portraits of George and Martha Washington, by John Trumbull, 1795.
Oil on canvas, 7″ × 6″.
These portraits were originally hung in the Washingtons' bedroom at Mount Vernon.
From the Lewis Collection,
National Museum of American History.

THE CALL: "NEW SCENES"

New scenes are opening upon us, and a very unexpected one, as respects myself is unfolding... When I bid adieu last to the theater of public life I thought it was hardly possible that any event would arise in my day that would enduce me to tread that Stage again. But this is an age of Wonders, and I have once more consented to become an Actor in the great Drama.

—George Washington to
Jonathan Trumbull
July 25, 1798

The only serious threat to George Washington's retirement was an appeal by President Adams to accept once again the appointment as Commander in Chief of the Army in face of what appeared to be imminent war with France. Washington consented and was soon drawing up plans for recruiting, organizing, and outfitting a provisional army. Fighting did break out at sea, but the army was never raised.

The exhibition also includes:

Commission issued to George Washington by President John Adams in 1798 in response to the quasi-war with France.
Lent by the Library of Congress.

General Washington's Letter Declaring his ACCEPTANCE of the Command of the ARMIES of the UNITED STATES published as a broadside *for General Information,* July 18, 1798.
National Museum of American History.

THE END: "TAKEN OFF THE STAGE"

Undeterred by snow and sleet on a December day in 1799, Washington took his usual ride to inspect his plantations, returning wet to the skin and crusted with ice. Within two days he was overcome by severe inflammatory swelling of the vocal chords. Following practices accepted for the time, his doctors applied salves to his throat and blisters and poultices of wheat bran to his legs and feet, and bled pints of blood from his body. The swelling continued; gradual suffocation brought death on December 14, 1799.

Figure 150
Bleeding instruments owned by Dr. Elisha Cullen Dick, one of the doctors in attendance during Washington's final illness.
Lent by Alexandria-Washington Lodge No. 22, A.F. & A.M.

On exhibit by courtesy of the Clerk of the Court of Fairfax County, Virginia, on July 9, 1982: The original copy of George Washington's Last Will and Testament.

Figure 151
Account of *The last illness and death of General Washington* by his secretary Tobias Lear, December 15, 1799. *The Great and Good Man is no more.*
Lent by the Clements Library, University of Michigan.

The exhibition also includes:

Medicine scales owned by Dr. Gustavus Richard Brown, one of the doctors in attendance at Washington's bedside.
National Museum of American History.

7

The following circumstantial account of the last illness and death of General Washington was noted by T. Lear, on Sunday following his death, which happened on Saturday Evening Dec. 14 1799, between the hours of ten and eleven. —

On Thursday Dec. 12 the General rode out to his farms about ten o'clock, and did not return home till past 3 o'clk. Soon after he went out, the weather became very bad, rain hail and snow falling alternately, with a cold wind. — When he came in I carried some letters to him, to frank, intending to send them to the Post Office in the evening. — He franked the letters; but said the weather was too bad to send a servant up to the office that evening. — I observed to him that I was afraid he had got wet, he said no, his great coat had kept him dry; but his neck appeared to be wet, and the snow was hanging on his hair. — He came to dinner without changing his dress. — In the evening he appeared as well as usual. —

A heavy fall of snow took place on Friday, which prevented the General from riding out as usual. — He had taken cold (undoubtedly from being so much exposed the day before) and complained of having a sore throat — he had a hoarseness, which increased in the evening; but he made light of it, as he would never take anything to carry off a cold, always observing, "let it go as it came". — In the evening, the papers having come from the Post Office, he sat in the room, with Mrs Washington and myself, reading them, 'till about nine o'clock, and

*And it is my express desire that my Corpse be
Interred in a private manner, without parade or
funeral Oration.*
  —George Washington, Last Will and Testament
                                           July 1799

**In accordance with his wishes, George
Washington's funeral was a simple service; he
saw himself once again a private gentleman
and did not want a state funeral. As a
concession to his national stature, his
survivors did allow a military procession and
a band, but for the most part only
Washington's family, friends, and neighbors
attended the service at Mount Vernon.**

**Washington was buried in a brick tomb in
the hillside below the mansion house. A
minister read the Episcopal Order of Burial
and members from local Masonic lodges
performed the traditional funeral rites of the
Order. As the service ended, cannon fire
echoed along the Potomac.**

Figure 152
Bill to *the Estate of the Late Genl George Washington
disceased* from Henry and Joseph Ingle of
Alexandria for a *Mahoy Coffin and silver plate
engraved; furnished with lace,* December 16, 1799.
Lent by the Mount Vernon Ladies' Association.

The exhibition also includes:

Announcement of George Washington's funeral.
Lent by the Mount Vernon Ladies' Association.

Contemporary account of George Washington's
funeral with a diagram of the procession, including
"The Body" and its attendents.
National Museum of American History.

Sword and scabbard owned by Col. Charles Little,
one of the honorary pallbearers at George
Washington's funeral.
Lent from a private collection.

Masonic apron worn at George Washington's
funeral service by one of the representatives from
the Alexandria Masonic Lodge No. 22.
*Lent by Alexandria-Washington Lodge No. 22,
A.F. & A.M.*

Watercolor of the tomb in which Washington was
buried on December 18, 1799, artist unknown,
early 19th century.
National Museum of American History.

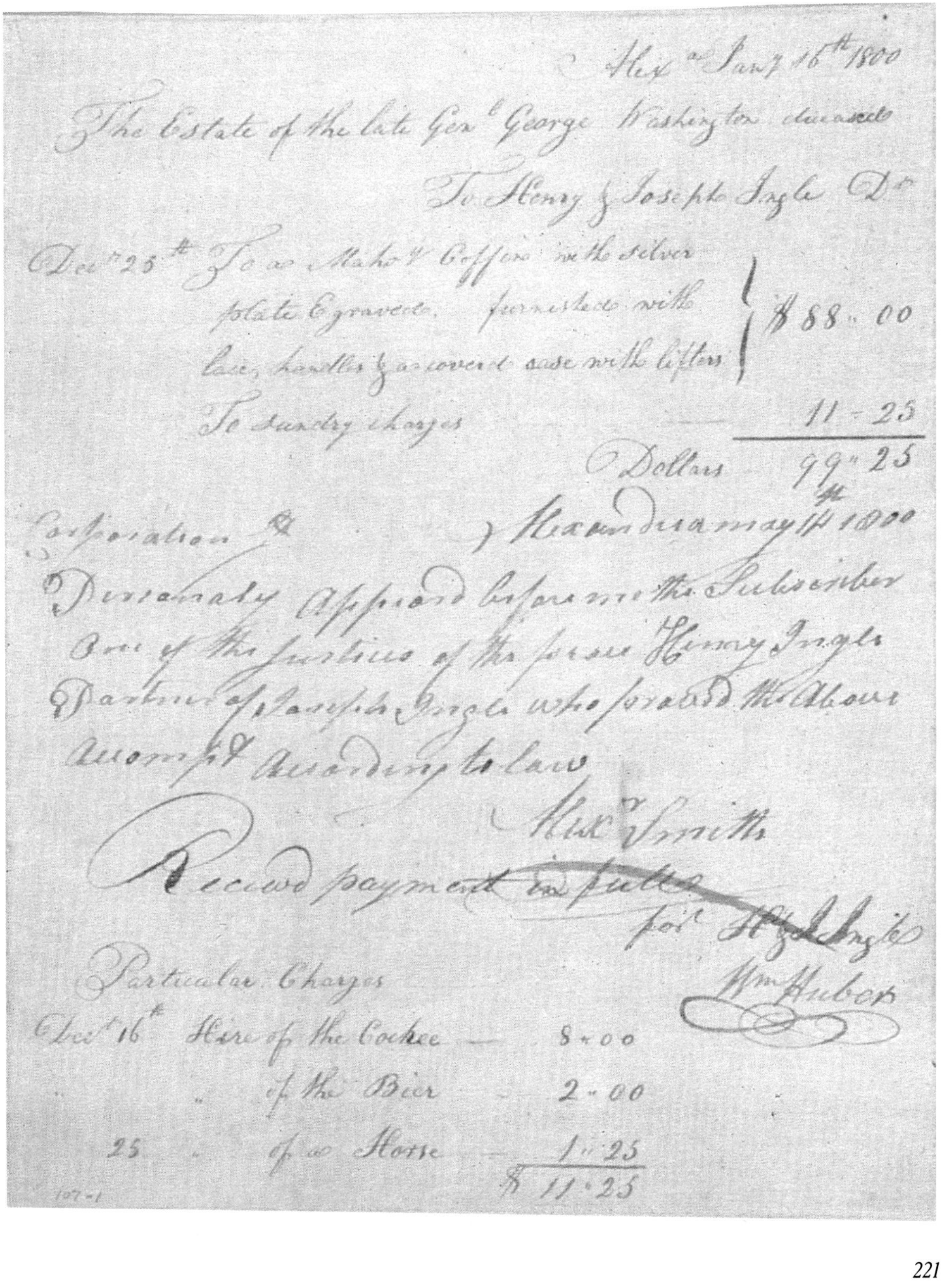

Alexa Jany 16th 1800

The Estate of the late Genl George Washington deceased

To Henry & Joseph Ingle Dr

Decr 25th To a Maho't Coffin with silver
plate Engraved. furnished with
lace, handles & a covered case with lifters } $88 . 00

To sundry charges ———————— 11 . 25

Dollars 99 . 25

Corporation &c } Alexandria may 14 1800

Personaly Appeard before me the Subscriber
one of the Justices of the peace Henry Ingle
Partner of Joseph Ingle who proved the above
account according to law

Alexr Smith

Reciewd payment in full

for H & J Ingle

Wm Hubert

Particular Charges
Decr 16th Hire of the Cochee —— 8 . 00
" of the Bier —— 2 . 00
25 " of a Horse —— 1 . 25
$ 11 . 25

THE AFTER-PIECE

The news of George Washington's death
spread quickly from state to state, announced
by special messengers and by black-bordered
papers. It sparked a wave of universal grief
and special commemoration which began in
Philadelphia with the formal day of mourning
on December 26 and continued by Presidential
proclamation until February 22, 1800.

When the news reached Europe, the
"Morning Chronicle" in London editorialized
that "His fame, bounded by no country, will be
confined to no age." In the harbor of Brest,
the flags of a British fleet were lowered to
half-mast. In France, First Consul Napoleon
Bonaparte announced Washington's death to
his army, ordered black crepe on all the flags
for ten days and personally delivered a
eulogy at the Temple of Mars. Funeral music
in Washington's honor was heard in Scotland,
the Netherlands, and elsewhere.

Personal expressions of lamentation at his
passing and praise of his virtues continued
long after the official commemoration and
eventually transformed Washington the man
into a godlike figure.

MOURNING

*Sorrow is depicted in the Countenances of all classes of
Citizen here . . . The houses and Shops were
immediately Shut. The Theatre is Shut. In Short I
believe there never was an Occasion where there was
more real Sorrow felt than upon this.*
     —Jonathan Smith, Esq., to Robert Frazer, Esq.
                    Philadelphia, December 18, 1799

The news of George Washington's death
plunged the nation into "general & deep
mourning." People throughout the country
organized memorial processions, bedecked
themselves with symbols of mourning and
delivered stirring eulogies and orations.

Figure 153
*High Street from the Country Market-place,
Philadelphia: with the procession in commemoration
of the Death of General George Washington,
December 26, 1799*, from *The City of Philadelphia*.
Etching and engraving by William Birch, 1800.
Lent by The Library Company of Philadelphia.

HIGH STREET, from the Country Market-place PHILADELPHIA:

with the procession in commemoration of the Death of GENERAL GEORGE WASHINGTON, *December 26th 1799.*

The exhibition also includes:

Original January 4, 1800, edition of the *Ulster County Gazette*, announcing the death of George Washington. This paper, published by Samuel Freer and Son in New York, was widely reproduced in subsequent years as a commemorative souvenir.
Lent by the Library of Congress.

Funeral Medal with the legend, *He in Glory, the World in Tears Ob.D. 14., 99.* Medals of this sort, identical in design to the Perkins medal but reproduced in cheaper metals, were worn as tokens of mourning by the general populace.
From the Ralph E. Becker Collection, National Museum of American History.

Mourning button with profile of George Washington, 1800.
National Museum of American History.

Ribbon with memorial portrait of George Washington, probably worn by mourners in 1800.
National Museum of American History.

Published text of the *Funeral Oration Occasioned by the Death of Gen. George Washington*, delivered by the Rev. Samuel Bayard in the Episcopal Church at New Rochelle, New York, on January 1, 1800.
From the Ralph E. Becker Collection, National Museum of American History.

An Eulogy on General George Washington Pronounced at Boston, pamphlet, 1800.
National Museum of American History.

Poetry Odes/On the death of/General George Washington/Who died December the 14, 1799, from a copybook by Betsy Lewis of Dorchester, Massachusetts, March 1800.
Lent by the Daughters of the American Revolution Museum; gift of Mrs. J. Gene Edwards.

Figure 154
Gold mourning ring containing a miniature portrait of George Washington, designed and engraved by M. Fevret Saint-Memin, 1800.
National Museum of American History.

Printed bandanna, *Sacred to the Memory of the Late, Great & Good George Washington*, with testimonials from the Minister of the French Court, the Court of Prussia, and eminent members of the English Parliament, c.1800.
National Museum of American History.

An engraving of General Washington by *W. Ridley from an Original Picture in the Possession of Saml Vaughan, Esq*, published by *European Magazine*, April 1, 1800.
National Museum of American History.

Reverse transfer print on glass depicting Columbia at Washington's tomb, c.1800.
From the Ralph E. Becker Collection, National Museum of American History.

Framed mourning embroidery with watercolor sections depicting two mourning goddesses around an urn with the inscription *Sacred to the Memory of the Illustrious Washington*, c.1800.
National Museum of American History.

Figure 155
Gold funeral medal set in a locket, designed and executed by Joseph Perkins of Newburyport, Massachusetts. These medals were offered for sale in the New England area as early as January 3, 1800.
National Museum of American History.

AN ELEGIAC POEM
ON THE DEATH OF
GENERAL GEORGE WASHINGTON;
Commander in Chief of the Armies of the United States.

Who died at Mount Vernon, Virginia, 14th December, 1799, aged 69 years.

DEDICATED TO THE CITIZENS
OF THE
United States.

The exhibition also includes:

Embroidered mourning picture commemorating
the death of George Washington, made by Hanna
Jackson Semple, c.1820.
Lent by The White House.

Sampler honoring George Washington,
embroidered by Olive Brown, c.1800.
National Museum of American History.

Chinese export porcelain sweetmeat dish decorated
with the tomb of Washington, from a service
ordered by his nephew Robert Lewis, c.1800.
Lent by the Kenmore Association.

APOTHEOSIS

His virtues and achievements can suffer no eclipse by a comparison with any mere man who has ever appeared on the great theater of the world.
— Rev. Asabel Hooker to Rev. James Muir
January 10, 1800

The grieving American people immediately began to transform George Washington into a godlike figure. They saw him as a majestic deity possessing infinite presence, power, wisdom, mercy, and goodness. They saw him as creator and as redeemer. They saw him surrounded by light, rising to sit in glory.

Figure 157
Liverpool ceramic pitcher with transfer print of *The Apotheosis of Washington*, c.1800.
From the Robert H. McCauley Collection, National Museum of American History.

Figure 158
The Apotheosis of Washington, reverse painting on glass made in China for the American market, early 19th century, $29\frac{1}{4}'' \times 27\frac{1}{2}''$.
Lent by the Museum of the American China Trade.

The exhibition also includes:

Commemoration of Washington, a depiction of the apotheosis of Washington, drawn and engraved by J.J. Barralet.
National Museum of American History.

Gray stoneware jug depicting the head of Christ, inscribed *George Washington Forever*, New York or Connecticut, 1810-1840.
Lent by the Henry Francis du Pont Winterthur Museum.

Washington was venerated by the people with religious fervor. Objects with an association —real or fancied— with him became revered as sacred relics.

The exhibition also includes:

Gold ring containing a bit of George Washington's coffin owned by Abraham Lincoln.
National Museum of American History.

Piece of George Washington's coat.
National Museum of American History.

Piece of the original coffin. When the body of George Washington was moved to the new tomb in 1831, bits of the old coffin became cherished keepsakes.
National Museum of American History.

Drinking glass preserved by generations of the McLane family because George Washington drank from it when he visited their home.
National Museum of American History.

Framed letter from George Washington, enclosing locks of his own and Martha's hair, sent to a Major Billings in 1783.
National Museum of American History.

Bricks from George Washington's birthplace. The house in which Washington was born at Popes Creek, Westmoreland County, Virginia, burned in 1780. The few bricks which survived the fire were carried off by souvenir collectors.
National Museum of American History.

Piece of George Washington's writing desk *accidently destroyed at the Richmond Capitol the winter of 1780-81.*
National Museum of American History.

Locks of George Washington's hair. Hair was a favorite memento of the great during the Victorian era and that of George Washington was especially treasured.
National Museum of American History.

MISSIONARY OF LIBERTY

Revered at home, George Washington became a symbol of liberty and revolution abroad. His name and his image were adopted by visionaries in Europe and in South America.

The exhibition also includes:

French creamware plate with blue painted decoration showing Washington in military uniform, late 18th century.
Lent by Phillip H. Tuseth.

Porcelain cup with hand-painted likeness of George Washington and gilt decorations, made by the Meissen Manufactory in Germany, c.1800.
Lent by The White House.

Ormulu clock decorated with standing figure of Washington, French, c.1810.
From Sheldon Arpad,
National Museum of American History.

Porcelain vase decorated with portrait of George Washington, French Empire.
National Museum of American History.

Ceramic chocolate mug with decorative floral motif and inscription *To Washington the Patriot of America,* English, 1799.
From the Ralph E. Becker Collection,
National Museum of American History.

Figure 159

Miniature of George Washington in gold locket.
This oil on ivory portrait was painted by Robert
Field in 1801 at the request of Martha Washington
as a memento for Bushrod Washington, a nephew.
Bushrod later sent the locket to Simon Bolivar in
recognition of his role in the revolutions in South
America:

*This portrait of the founder of American liberty in the
north, is given by his adopted son to him who has
achieved a like honor in the south.* Bolivar, known as
the *George Washington of South America,* wore the
locket as a symbol of honor.

*Lent by the Museo Bolivariano, Caracas, Venezuela,
through the courtesy of the Embassy of Venezuela,
Washington, D.C.*

GEORGE WASHINGTON 1732-1799